D1314688

BREAKTHROUGH IT

BREAKTHROUGH IT
Supercharging
Organizational Value
through Technology

Patrick Gray

BICENTENNIAL
1807
WILEY
2007
BICENTENNIAL

John Wiley & Sons, Inc.

Library of Congress Cataloging-in-Publication Data:
Gray, Patrick, 1977–
　Breakthrough IT : supercharging organizational value through technology / by Patrick Gray.
　　p. cm.
　ISBN 978-0-470-12484-0 (cloth : alk. paper)
1. Information technology–Management. 2. Technological innovations. 3. Organizational effectiveness.
I. Title. II. Title: Breakthrough information technology.
　HD30.2.G725 2007
　004.068′4–dc22   2007018190

Printed in the United States of America

10　9　8　7　6　5　4　3　2　1

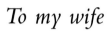

To my wife

Acknowledgments

This book would not have been possible without the clients of Prevoyance Group, Inc., who are far more than mere business partners, but teachers as well. Their struggles and successes were the inspiration for *Breakthrough IT*, and the proving ground for its concepts. I wish to thank Kathy Allen, Greg Buoncontri, Bridget Reiss, and Phil Stunt for their time and insights. Their guidance shaped and challenged my assumptions, as well as providing additional depth to this text.

My family has provided constant support, without which these pages would never have been possible. My parents instilled an accountant's business aptitude and an artist's creativity in their son, and provided wisdom that I appreciate more each day.

My wife, Meghan, has been a friend, critic, sounding board, and most important, a constant loving companion. She provided a much-needed "kick in the pants" to start Prevoyance Group, and her unending patience with long days on the road and long nights of writing helped make this book possible.

Contents

Contents

Contents

Contents

Preface

Breakthrough IT is the next step in the evolution of the corporate IT function. Since its inception, IT has focused on the technical aspect of its role, providing expertise and services with an increasingly mindful eye on doing so at a competitive price. While competing on cost has its merits, with the prevalence of outsourcing and market pressures, the time has come for a new way to manage IT, and that is Breakthrough IT.

While much of what Breakthrough IT entails is not necessarily new, and many leading CIOs, including those featured in this book, espouse several of its precepts, *Breakthrough IT* is the first book to look beyond the technologies that have been the focus of the IT industry. Instead of technology as the only tool of the IT organization, Breakthrough IT considers technology as only one method for instituting business change, and the CIO to be the primary person responsible for instituting process change, rather than a mere keeper of technology. Breakthrough IT combines several disciplines with the goal of making IT serve business objectives rather than provide and service tools. The idea is that IT should deliver and execute business strategy, not just provide a portfolio of commodity services.

While Breakthrough IT is a methodology of sorts, I am hesitant to present it as such. It is not something you can buy and install, or hire somebody to "do." It requires a fundamental change in the relationship between the CEO and CIO, and the relationship of the CIO and the IT organization to the rest of the corporation. Like anything beneficial, be it a trip to the gym or foundational changes in the way your company looks at its IT organization, it is difficult to implement and maintain, but offers astounding rewards. Those companies that are able to implement Breakthrough IT will have an unprecedented competitive advantage, as their IT department will be perceived as a value engine, whether it is successfully delivering strategic projects or designing and creating products for the end customer.

Similar to supply chain management, a formerly mundane aspect of business that suddenly became a source of competitive advantage for companies with the will and discipline to exploit it, Breakthrough IT will provide large dividends to companies willing to put in the effort required.

Perhaps the biggest competitive advantage of the Breakthrough IT organization is its focus on executing strategy. Today's business climate is one of unprecedented global change, be it in response to the new international playing field, the advent of disruptive technologies, or a changing labor market. The Breakthrough IT organization is inherently nimble, since it gets its direction from the senior executives of the corporation. Therefore, companies with Breakthrough IT will be able to change course quickly when required and maximize the potential of emerging business opportunities.

I have had the great privilege of working with many of the world's great companies, and those that aspire to greatness. The experiences I have acquired are the foundation for this book. I hope that you will find *Breakthrough IT* pragmatic, insightful, and actionable. I truly believe there is no better tool for creating a revolutionary IT function in your company.

Breakthrough IT Sections and Features

Breakthrough IT is designed to guide business leaders in transitioning their IT organization from an engineering or "utility-based" internal provider to a Breakthrough IT organization, capable of delivering predictable and measurable returns on IT investment. The first part of this book provides a methodology for transitioning IT from the old way of doing business into a Breakthrough IT organization. This part of the book will show CIOs how to develop process expertise within their organization, and provide guidelines for CEOs and CIOs to move their relationship from one of customer and vendor, to one of partners in fueling business growth.

The second part of the book covers the heart and soul of a Breakthrough IT organization: strategic projects. The Breakthrough IT organization has unburdened itself of its ongoing operations, transitioning the utility functions of IT to a vendor, be that an internal vendor or outsourcing to an external provider. The organization is then free to tie the strategic objectives of the business to a series of projects, each with a well-defined investment analysis providing a solid prediction of costs, and likely returns on the investment tied to each major project objective. As the Breakthrough CEO and CIO develop a track record of successes, returns can be predicted with increasing accuracy, and IT can become a powerful enabler of strategy. Tying all the major components of these projects to a defined target for business returns also adds an element of financial validity to the process. No longer are projects tracked based on percentages or "traffic light" charts that are easy to read but lack real substance behind the data. Rather, projects can be measured by what monetary value has been derived from the current level of investment. Like any other investment program, these projects will clearly indicate when they are delivering the required return, and a decision can be made to continue or terminate projects on a monetary basis with all the facts in the open, rather than relying on feeling and intuition.

The rest of the book describes where the proverbial rubber meets the road in a Breakthrough IT organization: successful execution of the strategic projects and influencing and leveraging the business changes they engender. The critical roles of the CEO and CIO in driving change management are spelled out, as well as detailed steps that must be taken to complete a postmortem on the project and determine where it was successful and where it failed once the implementation has been stabilized and organizational value is beginning to be derived. The Breakthrough IT shop is a learning organization, and even when investment objectives are not met, the results are critically examined to increase the likelihood of success of the next endeavor. In this manner, the corporation at large develops increasing process knowledge with each implementation, and increasing ability to accurately predict the returns on its strategic IT investment.

Each chapter provides a list of action points at its end. The action points provide a short list of items to consider, and concrete steps you can begin taking in your organization to transform its IT function into a true Breakthrough IT shop. The action points are followed by an executive summary. Use it to review the content from each chapter or to get an overview of the content in future chapters. The executive summary can also be used to quickly recall key points from each chapter and provide talking points to share with your colleagues.

Included in the book are several interviews with leading C-suite executives in various stages of implementing Breakthrough IT in their own companies. You will learn how IT is being used in their organizations, and gain insight from the front line across multiple industries, company sizes, and continents.

In addition, the author provides free articles and resources on his company's web site: www.prevoyancegroup.com. Prevoyance Group publishes a monthly newsletter, free to those who purchased *Breakthrough IT*. You can subscribe by visiting www.prevoyancegroup.com/subscribe-book/.

CHAPTER 1

Hell Freezes Over

IT Becomes a Key Component of Your Organizational Strategy

Marissa nearly chokes on her champagne when she feels a hearty slap on her back. Pausing a moment to compose herself and prevent any bubbly from escaping, she swallows and turns to see a beaming smile from her colleague Jim, the Chief Executive Officer (CEO) of Breakthrough Corp.

"I can't believe we've had such a successful product launch," his deep voice boomed, the excitement radiating through his usually stoic countenance.

"Two years ago when you approached me and said that IT could be the 'strategic weapon' that gets us to market more quickly and lowers our product development and support costs, I almost fell out of my chair. Who would have ever thought my CIO would be the 'ace in the hole' when it came to executing our strategic objectives?"

We live in one of the most interesting times in the history of the corporate Information Technology (IT) organization. Markets are continuing to expand globally, generating unprecedented opportunities for growth while at the same time imposing the threat of new and hungry competition, willing to deliver products and services better, cheaper, and faster. Labor pools have rapidly shifted, creating commodities out of what were once hot skill sets in a matter of months, and engendering positions and functions that were never dreamed of a few short years before.

At the same time, technology has "grown up" in the corporate world. As computers became affordable and reliable at the close of the 20th century, corporations rapidly adopted their use, seeing the promise in a tool that allowed for automation of routine tasks, and the ability to speed information gathering, processing, and analysis. The growing complexity of technology created the need for engineers, programmers, analysts, and eventually a cadre of managers to oversee this group of specialists. As technology further engrained itself within the corporation, this ragtag group crystallized into a specialized function, charged with maintaining the technology assets of the entire organization: IT as a corporate function was born.

More recently, IT has permeated nearly every corporation, large and small, even invading the C-suite, with the role of Chief Information Officer (CIO) becoming increasingly prominent. While the CIO title has been around for the better part of 30 years, it carries a fair amount of baggage, lacking the clout with the CEO that is generally held by the Chief Financial Officer (CFO) and Chief Operating Officer (COO). Many even joke that CIO really stands for "Career Is Over," indicating that the CIO position is as far as one can expect to advance when he or she has been "tainted" by a technology background.

Too often, even the best CIO is seen as a technologist, rather than a businessperson by his or her peers. The CIO is generally the last to be consulted on strategic initiatives, and is seen as providing a utility-like service to the corporation: a service that should be delivered at an increasingly high quality with an ever-decreasing budget.

The CEO is facing a similar dilemma. Productivity gains and competitive pressures have placed amazing demands on his or her leadership skills. Costs must be tightly managed and every modicum of market share increase must be battled for, against an increasingly hungry group of competitors in a global marketplace. Cost-cutting efforts, and the addition of new "business systems," either technology-based or process improvements such as Six Sigma or Lean, can help, but these can be easily applied by the competition. Cost cutting can go only so far until service levels and quality decrease, and organizations become pennypinchers to the point of becoming miserly in their dealings with customers.

Why Do You Need Breakthrough IT?

In this business environment, the IT organization has reached a crossroads. Commodity hardware and increasing availability of pre-packaged software functionality further the case for designing and managing IT as a low-cost utility. Should the CEO and CIO, with the help of other executives, strive for "best-in-class" utility status in their IT organization, or is there a way to transition IT from a utility that delivers cost savings, to a competitive weapon that delivers organizational value?

After the heady days of the technology boom, technology spending has been largely rationalized, and cost-cutting efforts have created effective utility-like shops. Companies strove to gain competitive advantage by further managing their costs; if you were similar in size and market to your competitor, but could get your product to the customer in a slightly less expensive manner, you could gain a competitive advantage. While this logic holds sound, most surviving companies have cut their costs to the point that further cost cutting no longer generates large competitive advantage, but rather diminishes service levels; the economic Law of Diminishing Returns comes into play as pictured in Exhibit 1.1.

Competitive advantage is no longer a simple matter of who can cut costs the most. As corporations at large, and in IT departments in particular, butt against the Law of Diminishing Returns, a better solution must be found. That solution is focusing on IT as a means to produce measurable business value, just as with any investment considered by the executives in a corporation. Banal statements from vendors about increasing return on investment (ROI) and the like must be replaced by a rigorous focus on measuring, tracking, and reacting to what value IT is producing. The companies focused on turning their IT

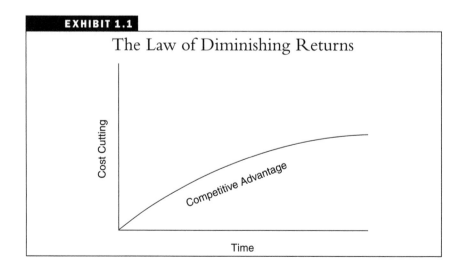

EXHIBIT 1.1

The Law of Diminishing Returns

Cost Cutting

Competitive Advantage

Time

department into a means to produce value will be leaps ahead of those continuing to focus on reducing costs. While your competitors spend time pondering the expenditure of each penny, your organization can be measuring the dollars produced by using IT as a strategic lever.

The need for the Breakthrough IT organization stems from the current corporate environment, and the "triple threat" of costs, commoditization, and the CEO/CIO relationship. A "utility" IT organization can never adapt to this new environment, and the Breakthrough IT organization provides an evolutionary response that both minimizes the operating costs of IT, and focuses on generating returns—a "one-two punch" to provide real competitive advantage.

The Triple Threat

The "triple threat" facing the corporate IT function is depicted in Exhibit 1.2. As each element increases its pressure on the IT organization, the impetus for action becomes increasingly critical. As this

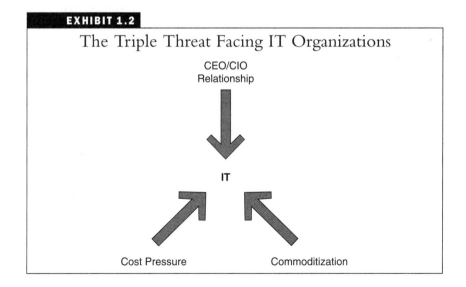

EXHIBIT 1.2

The Triple Threat Facing IT Organizations

CEO/CIO
Relationship

IT

Cost Pressure   Commoditization

pressure mounts, the CEO and CIO must take action to determine the future direction of the IT organization, before external pressures force their hand, precipitating a decision that may not be in the best interests of the corporation.

Threat: CEO/CIO Relationship

IT could use a lesson in "relationship marketing," especially when considering the working relationship between most CIOs and their counterparts in the C-suite. With the IT organization having originally been a group of technicians (engineers, programmers, developers, and the like), the CIO in many organizations has been groomed in an engineering environment. While C-suite colleagues were sharpening their leadership skills and managerial pedigree, the CIO often gained the perception of being an "über-technologist," frequently being derided as the geek who leads the other geeks. Many CIOs blindly follow this trend, considering themselves technologists first, and businesspeople a distant second.

This threat creates a customer/provider relationship between the CIO and other executives. The CIO is a manager charged with providing a service, to be invoked at the bequest of other groups within the organization, and as an ancillary or support function of these other organizations. The larger IT community of vendors and the IT media propagate this image, developing products touting "on demand" computing, or "utility computing." The result is that IT is effectively relegated to the role of an internal vendor, rather than a potential strategic partner within the organization.

When new product strategies are unveiled, or new sales and marketing programs are developed, the CIO rarely plays a role in the decision process, and often hears of these programs only when current systems fail to accommodate any new processes necessitated by the change in strategy or new products and services.

Conversely, most CEOs would rarely consider involving the CIO in the strategic decision-making processes. The über-technologist CIO comes to such discussions eager to jump to a recommendation on the latest technology or system that might be relevant to the topic at hand, often bringing solutions in search of a problem to the table. A systems focus adds little value to the formulation of a new strategy, and despite many vendors' claims to the contrary can hinder the execution of strategy.

This systems focus reinforces the role of IT and the CIO as a service provider, akin to an internal vendor. When a strategic direction has been chosen, the people aligned, and the policies and procedures put in place to execute it, only then is the CIO summoned to build any necessary systems around the processes.

Threat: Cost Pressure

From the mailroom clerk to the CEO, every employee of the modern corporation has felt the pressure to do more with less, and cut costs wherever possible. New corporate leadership often comes in wielding a cost-cutting axe, attempting to increase shareholder value by trimming organizational fat. This effect can be especially intense in IT organizations. Too many IT shops justify their existence based on uptime figures and service levels, rather than making a case that they deliver measurable business value, rendering IT an easy target for cost cutting and budget reductions.

As cost pressures mount, justifying budgets based on service levels becomes increasingly difficult. The inevitable question is, "What happens to our service levels if the budget is dropped by a few more percentage points?" Like most good managers, CIOs heroically struggle to meet targets with fewer resources, further cementing the view that IT funding can be continually cut until a "sweet spot" is found. In addition to ongoing operations, cost pressure impacts work carried out on a project basis. If a project is behind schedule or using more resources than were anticipated when the business justification for the project was completed, cost becomes an ever-greater concern.

CIOs generally rely on incomplete information about the state of such projects, measuring the work completed on various components of the overall solution, without a solid grasp on the overall status of the project. Projects are also rarely related to measurable business value, beyond the initial business case and benefit analysis, making it difficult to justify additional investment in the project when cost pressures mount. CIOs speak in a language of technical deliverables that conveys incomplete information to the CEO and CFO, who are more concerned with ROI than how many technical objects have been produced.

Threat: Commoditization

The IT industry has rapidly gone from a profession built on the technical knowledge of its employees, to a broad marketplace where technical skill and specialized software can be purchased at a commodity price, or even for free in the case of open source software. IT long enjoyed a measure of protection as it was a specialized area with strong "knowledge capital" stored in the many custom systems built by most large corporations over the years. In the 1980s, commoditization started in the software arena, with software vendors such as SAP creating software platforms with prebuilt business logic, providing an alternative to custom-built software for core business functionality at a significantly reduced cost to custom systems.

The wide adoption of package software brought about another change to the engineering specialist mentality, and the associated protections it provided to an entrenched IT group. If you know the latest word processing application and how to use it at one company, it will work in the exact same manner should you move to another company. In this same vein, developers and users alike of packaged business software can enter a new corporation with an established base of knowledge about their corporate systems before stepping through the door. Specialists who developed an archaic legacy system were no longer critical employees of the company once package software replaced highly specialized technical knowledge with knowledge of commodity software, which delivered the same set of standard functionality and processes in each installation.

Global markets, long bemoaned as causing the death of manufacturing jobs for many western countries, are now able to compete for IT jobs as well. The wide installed base of commodity business applications and easy availability of communications technologies have allowed increasingly higher-level work to be farmed out to the lowest bidder. This phenomenon has also engendered the development of large outsourcing organizations. As an IT function becomes commoditized, it favors economies of scale that often cannot be matched by an internal IT department. From marquee brands like IBM to newly formed companies in Cambodia, there is increasing competition to provide effective, commodity IT services at very low price points.

The Convergence of the Triple Threat

The confluence of the changing CEO/CIO relationship, cost, and commoditization has brought organizations to a critical decision point. The IT shop can continue to be an engineering/specialist organization, focused on providing technical services to various components of the business on an as-needed basis. Many CIOs have grounding in project management, or at least a reasonable amount of management and budgeting experience, so this role may come naturally. A "traditional" CIO reviews his or her roster of projects and ongoing operating costs, making a "pitch" to the CEO for sufficient funding. Focus in these meetings is often on how spending will help maintain the existing systems, and any new expenditures will offer enhanced technical capability to the organization, or replace aging platforms that have become costly to maintain. Other than perhaps in a general sense, fitting these expenditures into a context of a financial investment is rarely done.

Existing custom systems may necessitate the retention of the resources who initially built those systems, and if the CIO can maintain his or her IT organization in a reasonably cost-effective manner, he or she can delay any dramatic changes to their organization. Trapping specialized knowledge in legacy systems makes a strong case for an IT organization filled with the same specialists who originally developed, managed, and maintained the system, although this position is becoming increasingly risky with the arrival of commodity business software, and commodity technical skills available to enhance and maintain it.

Even the more "progressive" CIO who adopts commodity hardware and software, and runs his or her IT shop as a highly effective "internal vendor" is not immune to the effects of the triple threat. The technology press and many hardware and software vendors have encouraged this approach, trumpeting the cost savings of their various products. Terms like "On Demand" computing that imply the CIO and his or her organization is silently operating behind the scenes, to be invoked only when required—a "just-in-time" service organization of sorts that can be activated, or worse, "turned off" on the whims of external forces.

While specialized expertise and effective management of IT as a service may enhance the CIO's bargaining position in the near term, the triple threat is here to stay. When the CIO elects to take the aforementioned path, by the very nature of designing his or her organization to be an "internal vendor," he or she will be increasingly perceived as a vendor. This internal vendor, however, is saddled with uncompetitive high costs, versus a specialized external vendor. Employees must be retained to cover all the technical aspects of the business, and provided with healthcare, real estate (if you can call a cube farm "real estate"), payroll costs, and associated benefits. As the CIO navigates this burdensome cost structure, and becomes an increasingly competent internal vendor, the CEO eventually will make the natural comparison with external vendors who can assume control of some aspect of IT operations, or in many cases, assume the responsibility of the entire IT department by providing personnel, systems, and staffing.

Even the largest of corporations with the most effective IT departments can rarely compete with specialized external vendors, who can provide similar technical skills, purchased at a commodity price and at a lower cost through economies of scale. While your organization may need ten people to manage its network, a vendor may likely be able to serve five clients with a similar number of employees. The vendor can also call on shared internal staffing and knowledge resources on a massive scale, and on a true "on demand" basis. While any IT department can hire specialist consultants and contractors, it takes time to locate an appropriate party and bring him or her onsite. The external vendor, however, often has a specialist already on the payroll, to be deployed as needed within hours' notice instead of days or weeks. Competing with these organizations becomes nearly impossible when the CIO is in the role of a basic service provider.

From a CEO's perspective, if his or her CIO has cemented their relationship as a service provider, even a competent one, it makes the comparison with external vendors that much easier. IT generally is a very costly component of the corporate cost structure, and any reduction in that cost will be considered carefully. Like any other vendor, the CIO becomes only as good as his or her last "invoice."

Hell Freezes Over: IT Enables Strategy

Clearly, IT's attempt at being a low-cost service provider is a losing proposition to the CEO and CIO. With IT serving as a utility, the CIO is limited in his or her career progression. Even if the CIO manages a utility-like IT organization in a highly effective manner, that person will likely lack visibility to the strategic functions of the business, and be passed over for consideration for higher positions. For the CEO, IT is little different from any other utility. While electricity and phone service are critical to a company, the CEO expects that these utilities continue to function with complete reliability, and rarely scrutinizes these services unless seeking to cut their costs while maintaining a reasonable level of service.

What is needed then, is not striving to make IT cheaper, but to make IT generate measurable monetary returns to the business. Rather than each dollar of spending on IT being regarded as a sunk cost, if IT can generate proven returns on each dollar as an *investment* rather than a cost, IT becomes a powerful tool for generating competitive advantage. What is needed is a Breakthrough IT organization.

As business has evolved in the past several years, smart organizations have tended to flatten operations, streamlining reporting relationships, and breaking down traditional department structures. For example, in product engineering circles, engineers strove for a greater understanding of the manufacturing process, and made conscious decisions during the product design process to make products easier, quicker, and cheaper to manufacture. More recently, this concept has spread to other functions of the organization. Marketing was often left to develop marketing programs and campaigns after a product had been fully developed and production was in full swing. Current thinking, however, encourages companies to make marketing a critical aspect of product design, admonishing companies to build products for marketability *and* manufacturability. As depicted in Exhibit 1.3, Breakthrough IT is the next evolution in this process, and involves two key components: integrating IT with the design and execution of business strategy, and transitioning the corporate IT function from a center of

EXHIBIT 1.3

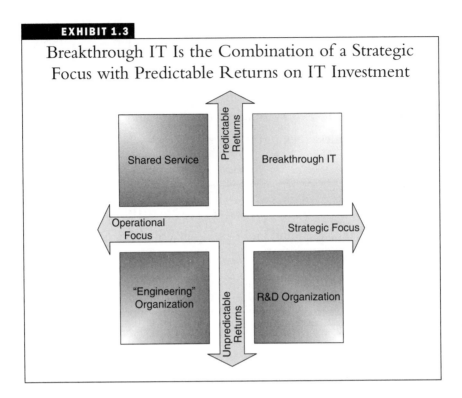

Breakthrough IT Is the Combination of a Strategic Focus with Predictable Returns on IT Investment

engineering expertise to a center of business process excellence founded on predictable returns on IT investment—in short, managing IT like any other business unit.

In the Breakthrough IT organization, IT is built into each venture the company embarks on. Products are designed with the input of each business unit, including IT. Rather than IT being recruited to build support for new products or business processes into inflexible systems after the fact, a cadre of process experts from the IT department designs processes and technology *into* the product from the outset. Instead of focusing on, and prematurely recommending, a specific technology, they design an efficient process first, and then look for areas in which technology could improve that process. The IT organization is less "geek," more business–process focused, from the CIO down to the most junior analyst. This process focus also makes IT increasingly "portable." By focusing on simplified and repeatable processes, IT operations can be moved to internal or external providers, and even across continents with relative ease.

ACTION POINTS

Action points provide concrete steps you can use to begin implementing ideas from this chapter. For this chapter, the action points are:

- Discuss the concepts of the Breakthrough IT organization with colleagues in the C-suite. Gauge their reactions and begin to gain conceptual agreement on the transition to Breakthrough IT. Do not strive for full commitment at this point; rather, get the ideas on the table for future consideration.

- Begin thinking about utility functions IT is currently managing internally. Future chapters will cover selecting which components of ongoing operations should be sourced and where, either internally or externally. The sooner you begin investigating options, the easier it will be to narrow down a detailed list of functions to transition away from your IT group's primary focus.

- Take a good look at your CIO's experience level and position in the organization. Does he or she have excellent management experience? Has that person managed a P&L (profit and loss)? Does he or she have a business process focus, or is that person an "über-technician?" Discuss this assessment and begin investigating coaching or leadership development options that will give the CIO the strategic acumen and

ACTION POINTS (CONTINUED)

leadership skills necessary to implement business strategy through IT.

- For the CIO, investigate current strategic imperatives for your company: new product developments or introductions, sales initiatives, competitive threats, and the marketplace in general. Begin to consider how process changes, facilitated by technology, may enable the strategic direction of your company and help it to react to competitive pressures and the changing business environment.

 EXECUTIVE SUMMARY

In this chapter, we discussed the origin of the CIO and the formalization of Information Technology as a corporate function. IT began primarily as an engineering function, comprised of people with a high level of technical expertise, tasked with maintaining complex and often highly customized systems. More recently, the trend in IT is to design the organization as a low-cost, "utility" function: delivering a service to other business units on an as-requested basis at the lowest possible cost. While this style of management has lowered overall IT spending in most organizations, the balance between low cost and acceptable service quality is being reached by most organizations. Further cost cutting only degrades the quality of service, thus limiting the competitive advantage that can be garnered by further cutting of IT costs.

This point of diminishing economic returns is combined with the "triple threat" facing IT: the CEO/CIO relationship, cost, and commoditization. The utility nature of most organizations has turned the CEO/CIO relationship into one of customer to vendor,

EXECUTIVE SUMMARY (CONTINUED)

and often the CIO has encouraged this relationship by attempting to make IT a low-cost internal service provider. The customer/vendor dynamic relegates the CIO and his or her IT organization into a simple service provider that can only compete on cost. The CIO is not a trusted peer of the CEO, and adds little value to the C-suite aside from how cheaply the CIO can provide a commodity service.

The threat of cost is that it is the primary benchmark by which a utility-style CIO and IT organization are judged. Internal organizations, be they IT or purchasing, have cost structures that simply cannot compete with large outsourcing firms that often can perform a business function at a lower cost and with higher quality due to the breadth of resources at their disposal.

Commoditization has helped the utility CIO cut costs by using standardized hardware, and increasingly commodity business software, that delivers prepackaged business processes and allows access to a large pool of talented people already experienced with the software. While software from companies such as Microsoft, Oracle, and SAP has provided cost advantage, competitors can purchase and implement the same solution, mitigating any competitive advantage incurred by the software itself, and the associated savings in maintenance costs.

This triple threat provides incentive for organizations to seek a method to use IT not as a low-cost utility, but as a business function that can generate measurable business returns. To build the Breakthrough IT organization, the CIO must effectively source all utility elements of the IT operation, either to an internal vendor or to an external provider. This frees the CIO to pursue a peer-level partnership with the CEO, using IT to speed the implementation and ROI generation of business strategy. The steps to accomplish this task are detailed in the remainder of this book.

CHAPTER 2

Up Periscope!
Ending the Focus on Continuing Operations

Nearly every worthwhile endeavor begins with a change in mindset, and building the Breakthrough IT organization is no different. The first step on the journey to a more effective IT group that actually generates measurable returns, rather than being yet another drag on the P&L, is seeing IT as a "business" in and of itself, and as a venture capital organization. The business element of your Breakthrough IT organization seeks to minimize its ongoing, non-investment costs, while the venture capital component of the organization explores potential strategic projects through an active and ongoing collaboration with other executives in the firm.

The first step in building this organization is reducing your company's focus on ongoing IT operations. This aspect has long been the primary, and in some cases, the sole focus of IT. Keeping the networks running and the myriad little lights in the server room blinking a steady green are important to business continuity, but should not be the primary concern of a C-level executive. This chapter centers on transitioning the focus of IT away from continuing operations, with the objective of freeing the organization to use IT as a competitive weapon by implementing strategic projects.

This is not a task to be undertaken lightly. The dynamics of the relationship between the CEO and CIO will often change during this transition, and both executives must make the mental shift from viewing the CIO and IT as an operational function to seeing the role of each as implementing strategy. This transition will also be uncomfortable for many CIOs. At best, the CIO has been treated as an independent service provider, responsible primarily for managing a budget and controlling the costs of the IT organization. The CIO of the Breakthrough IT organization will be tasked with far more. He or she will leave the comfort of implementing technical solutions, and be required to take the strategic vision of the CEO and work with other executives to implement that vision. He or she will be applying technology as a means to that end, rather than being judged solely on the technologies implemented and the costs incurred to do so. While the risk of failure for the CIO is higher in the Breakthrough IT organization, the title of CIO no longer can be associated with the old joke that CIO really means "Career Is Over." The role of CIO now is both a proving ground and a role that has enough of a strategic element to make it a potential steppingstone for higher positions in the executive suite.

A Brief History of IT

The Dark Ages of the Mainframe

Before delving into the details of transitioning your IT organization's focus from continuing operations to strategic projects, a brief investigation into how IT arrived at its current operational role and why this situation is becoming untenable is in order.

Even in modern corporations, IT is often compared to a manufacturing organization. This comparison is appropriate, as IT was effectively a specialized manufacturing function when technology first began appearing in corporations. Mainframe hardware was similar to heavy manufacturing equipment, both in the physical sense and in how it was managed.

Physically, mainframes were bulky, hot, and noisy machines. They required special facilities isolated from the rest of the organization, just as a manufacturing floor does. In its nascent stages, corporate computing consisted of processing jobs in a sequential manner. Like manufacturing, jobs were scheduled and timed, and various users were allocated a timeslot for their jobs before the mainframe had to be "retooled" and prepared for the next job.

Again, like a piece of manufacturing equipment, the mainframe required specialized engineers to maintain the machinery, and determine how a computing job would be input to the machine, scheduled, and executed. The engineer did not need to know the how or why of the job being executed beyond the extent required to perform the job and provide an output the requestor could use. Like manufacturing, IT technicians were drawn from engineering and scientific disciplines, rather than from corporate finance or management.

Administering these computing jobs was a passive activity. IT had a given amount of computing capacity, which would effectively sit idle until some business user required a job to be added to the queue for IT to schedule and execute. The goal of the managers of this function was to have their computing capacity 100 percent used at all times, with the shortest possible queue of jobs waiting to be executed. In effect, they were tasked with efficiently managing production.

Most companies also had proprietary hardware, operating systems and custom software managed by their IT department, just as many manufacturing operations had a customized assembly line or tooling for the particular product being produced. While an IT engineer certainly could learn the nuances of another system, the learning curve was steep, and any competitive advantage obtained through custom applications was difficult to duplicate without inside knowledge.

Competitive advantage in the mainframe era of IT was generated by having the ability to purchase enough computing capacity, and the managerial skills to ensure that capacity was 100 percent used. In addition, customized hardware, software, and "manufacturing prowess" played a key role. If you were better at managing your capacity than the next organization, or had the best engineers who could create more effective systems than your competition, IT became a competitive advantage.

Power to the People: Desktops

The arrival of desktop computers may have broken the stranglehold of the mainframe on corporate computing, and reduced the central role of IT in managing the scheduling and execution of computing jobs, but this change did little to affect the centralized manufacturing aspect of IT as client server computing became mainstream. Rather than a central mainframe controlling all access to job processing, computing power could be split between the central control of the IT organization and the individual computing power present on each desktop. While IT no longer required specialized mainframe engineers, an army of lower-skilled support staff was required to install, maintain, and support desktop users.

The arrival of the desktop also brought about one central element of the Triple Threat introduced in the last chapter: commoditization. As everything from word processing and spreadsheets to enterprise business applications became standardized and universally available, the "manufacturing savvy" element of IT organizations was reduced. Custom code went from a tool of competitive advantage to a hindrance. If your company was not using standardized business applications, you risked high costs in maintenance, and an inability to communicate with business partners through standardized channels such as EDI and XML.

The commoditization of hardware and software reduced the costs of acquiring IT, and the dependence on highly specialized engineers. No longer was the ability to control and schedule computing capacity central to generating competitive advantage. Rather, two tools were available to outwit competitors: doing things cheaper, and implementing the same technology quicker. In this environment, management of IT resources became more critical than engineering acumen. With the same tools available to everyone in the form of commodity hardware and software, if you could pick the right mix of tools, integrate them quickly, and streamline their management, your IT shop could carry the day.

Client server computing added many elements of complexity to IT, spreading computing capacity all over the organization and giving users unparalleled access to computing resources without directly involving IT. However, IT management still remained centrally focused on purchasing the correct amount of computing capacity, making sure all resources were 100 percent used while ensuring there was no "job queuing" due to inadequate technology resources.

We Can't Go on Like This

A legacy of managing IT like a manufacturing operation, and the availability of commodity hardware and applications, has caused many CEOs and CIOs to make the decision to manage their IT shop as a glorified manufacturing job shop. IT would passively wait for "permission" from a business group to request some functionality. IT then would shop for some combination of commodity hardware or software, and determine the cost to buy and implement the necessary technology. In some cases, CIOs presented a "menu" of options to their counterparts, who would select a particular option. Like a restaurant, the activities "in the kitchen" were invisible to the consumer of the services, and as long as the result was satisfactory, little concern was paid to anything other than providing acceptable quality at a reasonable cost.

This is similar to what happened to manufacturing in many high-cost countries in North America and Europe. Manufacturing did one thing: It built products at an acceptable level of quality with minimal intervention from the business that was tasked with marketing and selling those products. For years, this arrangement was satisfactory, but the sudden availability of a reasonably skilled manufacturing workforce

at a modicum of the cost completely changed the dynamic. Manufacturing had made itself such a perfectly managed "internal vendor"
that it was simple to source this function from outside the company.
How does IT avoid this fate? We "open the kitchen" and provide more
value than just delivery of an acceptable service at the lowest possible
price.

Shifting the Focus: Moving IT from Service Provider to Strategic Asset

The long-term objective of the Breakthrough IT organization is to
shift the focus of IT from providing a commodity service at the lowest
possible cost to helping the company execute on its strategic objectives.
The next chapter covers the details of this shift in focus, but IT cannot
become a strategic asset if it continues to have much of its energy and
resources devoted to supplying a low-cost utility-like service.

Traditionally, continuing operations were the primary focus of IT,
based on the history and legacy of IT organizations, current management practices, and the IT marketplace. Software vendors push
"solutions" to problems that are based primarily on the application
of technology and, despite elaborate descriptions and marketing
materials, are little more than a Madison Avenue–developed snake
oil pitch, with vaporous claims of high ROI with little factual backup.
Most CIOs followed an 80/20 rule, spending approximately 80
percent of their budgets (and more importantly, 80 percent of their
"mind time" and management focus) on continuing operations, and
the other 20 percent or less on what could be legitimately considered
strategic activities. For now, let us consider anything related to ongoing

operations as the nonstrategic component of IT. The first stage of the transformation to Breakthrough status is eliminating the utility aspects of the business and mitigating its impact on budgets, but more importantly, minimizing the "mental focus" expended on keeping the IT lights on.

Separating the ongoing operations of your business also allows you to view IT from a business process perspective, separating the processes from the technology that facilitates their execution. While a particular technology, such as security hardware and software, may be critical to the business, it is not associated with any particular business or strategic process. These functions often distract the focus of the technology organization, and serve to further distance the CEO and CIO. Security may be critical to the company, but is a process that can effectively be left to internal or external experts, allowing the CIO to focus on technology that is applied to critical and strategic business processes, thus finding a common language between the CIO and his or her peers in the executive suite. This process-centric view of the world is covered in further detail in Chapter 7, but for now serves as a reminder that an IT function may be critical in that it serves a key infrastructure function that must have a high degree of reliability. However, that factor alone does not exclude it from being categorized as an ongoing operational activity.

While the mere mention of outsourcing or any sourcing decision is often met with much angst by the CIO, a change in perception is needed. Just as commodity manufacturing is a difficult business to justify retaining internally, commodity IT processes should be similarly targeted for a sourcing change to allow the CIO to "up market" his or her IT organization, and provide higher-value strategic results to the corporation. The CIO should embrace the analysis and disposition of commodity services as a chance to save money and shed distractions. Outsourcing is no longer innovative or a discussion that can be avoided. The Breakthrough CIO must address and justify all his or her sourcing decisions with a focus on strategic value, rather than a perceived imperative of keeping the "IT Empire" in one piece.

Calling Sherlock Holmes: Finding Continuing Operations

There are three basic areas within most corporate IT functions to search for continuing operations:

1. Business processes that do not have any direct impact on the end customer of the corporation. This is the person who actually buys goods and services from the company, not the internal customer or client nomenclature that is popular in a utility-based IT shop.

2. The annual IT budget and the detailed actual costs that comprise it.

3. Activities that have dedicated internal support staff with their own team structured around a technology-based function (i.e., a network operations team or security management team).

The goal of investigating these areas is to identify functions that are eligible for a sourcing change. If an activity does not provide any customer touch points, constitutes an ongoing operational cost, or functions largely as a standalone entity, a sourcing change will get the function off the CIO's radar, allowing him or her to focus on enabling business strategy and transitioning toward a Breakthrough IT organization. Many CIOs balk at any suggestion of a sourcing change, be it a decision to outsource or setting up internal "providers" who can independently manage a specific function. The decision to proactively make sourcing changes prevents making a hasty move, driven by other C-suite executives who may focus on cost as the only criterion for a sourcing change. Well before the topic of outsourcing is broached between the CEO and CIO, the CIO should be analyzing his or her organization, and developing a sourcing plan that is thorough and carefully considered, lest he or she be forced to make a short-term sourcing change that causes more problems for the CIO and the organization as a whole in the long run.

IT organizations often get the most exposure to different elements of a business, save perhaps for the CEO. Technology has permeated every aspect of business over the past several decades, from complex logistics systems, to executive dashboards that give CEOs a snapshot of corporate performance, to systems to track the performance and pipeline of field sales representatives. From this vantage point, it is surprising that IT has not embarked on a formal movement to focus itself away from a detailed understanding of technology, to a detailed understanding of business processes.

From a revenue and "sensitivity" standpoint, the processes most critical to businesses' success are those that have direct contact with an end customer. While invoicing is certainly not a very exciting process, a complex or incorrect invoice can do more damage to customer perception than years of expensive marketing programs. However, IT security and the dramatic battles against hackers and crackers make great front-page headlines, but save for the case where total security failure compromises customer information, security policies and procedures concern a customer far less than a recurring overcharge on an invoice that requires monthly calls to resolve. Security is more of a procedural activity than one tied directly to customer interaction. Exhibit 2.1 provides some examples of customer-facing processes that likely have a high element of IT involvement.

If your IT operation has done a good job in the past of documenting the processes where it has applied technology, identifying areas in which end customers are impacted should be easier. In addition, any organizational process improvements, such as Six Sigma or the like, may have process documentation that will serve this purpose. If this documentation does not exist, an effort to analyze current IT systems and determine their associated business processes can be undertaken at a basic level, or a more detailed analysis may be performed. A more in-depth analysis will help when identifying opportunities for strategic IT projects as your technology organization transitions to Breakthrough status, but to determine processes eligible for outsourcing at this stage of the game, only a basic investigation is required.

Perhaps the simplest place to begin the search for continuing operational activities is the annual IT budget and any associated line item costs that comprise it. Items that appear regularly on the budget, year after year, are likely a clue to the existence of an ongoing cost associated with utility operations. Any area in which you have recently investigated reducing costs, or looked to an outsourcing provider, obviously falls within this category, as well as more subtle costs such as recurring costs for software licensing or infrastructure upgrades that are a function of organizational growth rather than strategic spending. Investigating budget items also has an advantage in that it can identify the ongoing operational area, and the hard monetary cost associated

EXHIBIT 2.1

Common Business Processes with Extensive IT Involvement and High Customer Impact

Process	Customer Impact
Call Centers	Call centers are usually the front line of customer contact. Operators who complain to customers about poor systems or do not have access to the right information at the right time instantly spoil a customer's impression of a company.
Invoicing	The invoice is the last statement your company makes to a customer, and can sour an otherwise positive experience or leave a good impression even after a less-than-successful sale.
Marketing Systems	Automated marketing systems have a direct and obvious impact on customers. Poorly designed communications, or flooding a customer's phone, inbox or mailbox have a direct impact on the customer.
Sales	Sales reps with up-to-date product information and lead times create a company that is able to deliver on what it promises.
Self-service Applications	A self-service application for checking order status, viewing invoices, or finding answers to common questions can create a positive impression and increase customer service while decreasing costs. Always design these systems with the customer in mind, and do not use them for data gathering tools or make them so complex they are ignored or create an unfavorable impression.

with it. In conducting a thorough analysis of processes that should be outsourced, cost is an obvious criterion that will play a role in the sourcing decision.

The organizational chart of the IT department is another key item in the hunt for ongoing operations. Several utility functions have dedicated staff supporting them, such as network operations or hardware support. When investigating these functions, the CIO should make a note as to how effectively each of these functions can stand on its own. If IT has a particular team that covers a function such as network operations that is able to manage its own budget, develop and execute an operational plan, and meet its service targets at a competitive cost with minimal input from the CIO, that function has effectively been "outsourced" to an internal provider. The key factor in determining which functions are operating at that level is the level of input and interaction the CIO must provide that group. If the function meets the 2 percent rule, requiring less than 2 percent of the CIO's time each year, including budgeting, planning, execution, and "troubleshooting," then sourcing that function outside the company to an external provider should be considered only if there are substantial cost savings.

Functions within the IT organization that constantly require attention, or present the occasional but time-consuming "firefight," must also be added to the list of potential functions for a sourcing change. A function that operates in a standalone manner is not immune to a sourcing change if once a year it distracts the attention of the IT group or the organization as a whole, derailing all other activities and requiring complete focus.

The objective of this investigational exercise is to develop a matrix of business processes IT contributes to, their impact on the end customer of the business, complexity, and cost. In addition, soft criteria such as CIO and non-IT "mindshare," the extent to which the process

EXHIBIT 2.2

Sample Sourcing Matrix

Process	Customer Impact	Complexity	CIO Mindshare	Strategic or Operational	Internal Org?	Outsource/ Insource/ Internal
Network Operations	Low	Med.	Low	Op.	Yes	Insource
Desktop Support	Low	Low	Low	Op.	Yes	Outsource
Outbound Call Center	High	Low	Med.	Strat.	Yes	Internal

requires management or attention from the CIO and business leaders, should be noted and quantified. A sample of such a matrix is presented in Exhibit 2.2.

Changing the Source: What to Do with Continuing Operations

When the matrix in Exhibit 2.2 is completed, sourcing alternatives can be compared. For any ongoing operational process, two options exist: insourcing and outsourcing. Despite the temptation to maintain the status quo and keep the CIO as the primary manager of a utility process, the goal of this activity is to "clear the decks" of the IT organization to allow for a focus on business strategy first, and cost savings a close second. Remember that the Breakthrough IT organization strives not to be a low-cost provider, but to deliver consistent, quantifiable returns on investment. If a sourcing decision has costs and service levels that are roughly equal, preference should always be given to the option that frees the CIO and IT's strongest employees to execute business strategy.

Keeping the Work in House: Insourcing

Insourcing is often overlooked as an option when deciding what to do with continuing IT operations, often due more to organizational control issues rather than any particular difficulty with implementing the process. Simply put, insourcing is establishing an internal organization with its own budget, independent management, and management targets and objectives, effectively creating an independent service company within the larger corporation. Like any sourcing decision, the primary objective of insourcing is to remove ongoing operational activities from the "corporate radar," and allow executives to focus IT on delivering strategic objectives. Exhibit 2.3 summarizes the key components of an insourced operation.

Insourcing keeps work and employees in-house versus using an outsourcing provider, but it is critical that any insourced function be treated as an independent organization. The managers of the insourced "company" must be treated independently, both in their interactions with their "customers" and in terms of having the freedom to make operating decisions. Creating a new organization but continuing to maintain old reporting relationships and management styles will not provide the key benefit of a sourcing change: eliminating ongoing operations from "management radar." Ideally, quarterly objectives for the insourced organization will be established and reviewed, and the management of the insourced function will otherwise be given full operational freedom. Just as is the case with an external vendor, this freedom comes with an assumption that not meeting established targets

EXHIBIT 2.3

Components of an Insourced Operation

Capability	Description	Benefit
Defined Budget	Each insourced organization should operate as a "company within the company," with a defined budget allocation process. Once the budget is allocated, the insourced organization should have the freedom to manage it independently and be awarded for cost controls. Budget increases outside the regular budgeting process should be awarded only in extreme circumstances.	Costs for each insourced component are clearly defined in advance.
Independent Management	Sticking to the company-within-the-company theme, an insourced organization should have trusted management that can operate with little input from corporate management as a whole. Management of an insourced operation should be free to spend its budget as it sees fit, and manage all its interactions with internal "customers."	High-quality management of the insourced operation frees the CIO's and CEO's attentions to focus on executing strategic objectives. Management of the insourced organization can focus on daily firefighting with little input from leadership. Independent management also allows for leadership and talent development within the insourced organization.
Targets and Objectives	Defined service levels and operational criteria should be established, along with appropriate metrics for their measurement at budgeting time.	Defined targets and objectives provide a well-known framework for judging and evaluating the effectiveness of the insourced operation.

will result in the replacement of the insourced function by outsourcing it or forcing a management change.

The "Big O"—Outsourcing

An entire book can be easily penned on outsourcing and its merits or detriments on a corporate, social, and political level. For the purposes of the Breakthrough IT organization, outsourcing is simply another option in determining how to disposition continuing operations. One benefit of outsourcing versus developing an insourced operation from a Breakthrough IT perspective is that independent management is virtually guaranteed in most circumstances. The outsourcing provider is generally an entirely separate corporation, and its management infrastructure is likely located in a different geographic area, perhaps oceans away. An outsourced function can be easily eliminated from the C-suite radar, assuming the outsourcing provider is competent and provided with a defined and measurable set of targets and objectives. Similar to an insourced operation, if the outsourcing provider consistently fails to meet these targets, it is time to consider another provider.

An outsourcing provider should also be an expert in the function they will be managing. Hiring the "bargain-basement" provider may appeal to corporate finance, but if you cannot eliminate management attention on continuing operations through the outsourcing arrangement, it will prove more costly in the long run. Whatever the sourcing decision, recall that the Breakthrough IT organization is never only a low-cost provider, and your sourcing decisions should focus on providing effective service levels and allowing IT's focus to shift to strategy and execution, rather than just lowering IT costs.

Preparing for a Sourcing Change

After identifying ongoing operations and determining which are eligible for a sourcing change, the CEO and CIO should jointly review the list of process groups, and create a defined set of targets and objectives for each function. Potential managers for an insourced operation should be investigated, and actively "pitch" their services against potential outsourcing vendors. A determination of startup costs associated with the sourcing change should be undertaken, accounting for the organizational and process changes that will facilitate transferring a process from direct management by the IT group to management by an independent entity.

During the vendor selection process, ensure that the focus stays primarily on the ability of the sourcing entity to meet your targets and objectives at a competitive cost. In the case of similar costs, some sample factors that may sway decision making one way or another include:

- Insourcing provides better possibility for leadership development, since the manager of the insourced operation will largely operate as if running his or her own company or business unit. The risk is that the CIO will retain control over the insourced operation and thus eliminate the primary benefit of the sourcing change.

- Insourcing offers obvious geographic benefits, but with that retains fixed costs such as facilities, employee benefits, other HR costs, and the associated headaches, as opposed to a truly independent organization.

- Outsourcing a continuing operation that adds no strategic value to the organization due to, for example, maintenance of a dying technology may make more sense than insourcing, since training and hiring can focus on more critical matters rather than expending the effort to support a dying technology.

- "Switching costs" may be higher with an external provider, since management can be replaced in an internal provider without changing the rest of the organization. However, if you are not receiving the promised service from an outsourcing provider, make your concern known, as there is always a possibility of instituting a change in the management of your account there as well.

The organizational changes, and changes to the "people process" of your organization associated with a sourcing change, will be felt in both the IT department and areas of the business that interact with the IT shop. IT has to deal with transitioning continuing operations, and a marketing effort to let the rest of the organization know the old role of utility service provider is a distant secondary effort to providing process and operational excellence. This change is a critical component of the transition to the Breakthrough IT organization, and will be fully considered in Chapter 4, "Clear the Benches: Take Your IT Shop from Dysfunction to Dynamo."

Once the decks are clear of ongoing operations, the foundation is laid for achieving Breakthrough status. The headaches and "mindshare" required to solve ongoing operational problems and engage in "fire fighting" should gradually become a thing of the past as new sourcing providers, be they internal or external, take over the management of these processes. With the CIO and the IT organization freed from these processes, the next step is a full marketing assault, changing the organizational perception of IT from a low-cost operational provider to a comprehensive provider of strategic knowledge and execution capabilities.

ACTION POINTS

Action points provide concrete steps you can use to begin implementing ideas from this chapter. For this chapter, the action points are:

- Honestly assess your IT organization within the framework of the *Brief History of IT*, discussed earlier. Where does your organization fit, and what can you do to move it toward Breakthrough status?

- Ensure your IT organization is fully using commodity hardware and services. This allows for easier sourcing decisions, and enables a change in focus of IT personnel from technical engineering experts to process experts.

- Begin shifting your view of IT from a series of technologies to a series of business processes enabled or augmented by technology.

- Begin the search for continuing operations. During the coming weeks, consider each aspect of your IT organization and begin categorizing and identifying each activity that represents continuing operations.

- After locating and documenting processes that represent continuing operations, determine relevant targets, objectives, and measures that each area must meet to provide high-quality service to the corporation. Begin looking for new sourcing options that can meet these targets and objectives at an acceptable cost. Remember to consider both insourcing and outsourcing as viable options, as long as each alternative allows the operation to be "hands off," requiring a minimum of input from the CEO and CIO.

ACTION POINTS (CONTINUED)

- Begin to think about appropriate "people processes" that will transition your IT employees away from roles based on technical expertise and move them toward cross-functional process experts.

 EXECUTIVE SUMMARY

In this chapter, we began with a "Brief History of IT" from the mainframe era to the eventual commoditization of hardware, software, and the skills that maintain them. This history traces the origins of IT as an engineering and technical competency center, focused on completing tasks rather than on business processes, a hangover from the early days of computing. This task and technology focus has moved IT rapidly toward the same fate as manufacturing, with dedicated organizations often in low-cost geographic locations able to provide commodity services at a dramatically lower cost than many traditional IT organizations. The alternative to falling victim to commoditization is the transition to Breakthrough IT status.

The first stage in achieving Breakthrough status is shifting organizational focus away from continuing operations: tasks that maintain IT infrastructure and provide an "on-demand" service for other business units, rather than proactively seeking to generate business value. Finding these ongoing operations and the criteria used to determine whether a particular process qualifies as continuing operations depends on whether the process impacts the end customer, is a recurring budget item, has a dedicated organizational support structure built around the task (i.e., desktop support or network operations), or some combination thereof.

Once continuing operations have been identified, the goal of executive leadership is to transition them off the "management radar,'' moving these tasks to an organization that can manage their budget, daily activities, and meet a defined set of targets and objectives. The focus in any sourcing decision should be whether these tasks can be eliminated as a recipient of constant management attention first, and using the lowest-cost provider a distant second.

Two primary options are presented for a sourcing change: insourcing and outsourcing. Insourcing is the process of establishing a ''company within the company'' with its own dedicated management structure and budget. This option minimizes the impact on current employees, and mitigates any issues with sending IT tasks to an outside vendor. This also creates the potential for using an insourced operational area to groom management and leadership talent. If poorly implemented, however, the potential for ongoing headaches and micromanagement is strong when the insourced organization is physically close. Costs are generally higher for insourcing, since fixed costs such as office space and employee benefits are not transitioned to another provider, and the economies of scale that are generally present when using an outsourcing organization dedicated to a particular task or function are not realized.

Outsourcing moves the tasks in question to an outside provider, often transitioning jobs, equipment, and physical proximity to that provider. This physical ''division of duties'' can further cement the shift in management focus from continuing operations to a strategic focus, and get the company out of a dying business, such as maintaining legacy applications that soon will be replaced. Either decision requires careful management of the associated personnel issues and ''people processes'' that will surround any sourcing decision, and ongoing monitoring of whether the sourcing provider continues to meet established targets and objectives.

CHAPTER 3

ET Phone Home

Stop Talking IT and Start Talking Strategy

One of the worst "hangovers" from the mainframe era of computing is the typecast role of the CIO as a technologist, the engineer first and business leader a distant second. Like many other expert resources, the perception of the CIO as a technology expert has led his or her peers to consult him or her only when specific input is required in the CIO's area of expertise. Contrast this to the role of the CEO, CFO, or COO. While the latter two have expertise centering on finance and operations, they are primarily tasked with executing business strategy in their particular areas. If a new market is to be exploited, the CFO determines the financial risks and rewards, and how to finance the entrée into the new market. In a similar vein, the COO determines how the company's operations will change to accommodate the new market, perhaps by introducing new products and planning their production, or by modifying the supply chain to facilitate transactions with new customers in that particular market. Contrast these roles to that of the CIO, where he or she is not tasked with planning how technology resources can be leveraged to enter a new market; rather, the CIO is generally called after battle plans have been drawn, employees mobilized, and execution of the strategy long since started. The CIO is called in as an expert when something stops working, or when bandages must be applied to an existing system. It is time for this role to change.

There is an entertaining "chicken-and-egg"-type debate that can be recounted over a favorite beverage relating to whether the CIO was always a technologist, and the archetype of "über-Geek" was a result of this perception, or whether CIOs have struggled mightily against the stereotype only to be relegated to the technologist role due to unfounded assumptions by other executives. While circumstances at a particular organization may play into this perception, and the technology marketplace does CIOs no favors in reducing their perception as technology experts, much of this change in perception is in the hands of the CIOs themselves.

The perception of the CIO as a technologist drives a wedge between the CIO and his or her fellow C-suite executives. This element of the triple threat discussed in the first chapter is a key obstacle to creating the Breakthrough IT organization. The annals of management history are littered with various trends and fads that looked good on paper and were implemented with all the best intentions, but gradually fizzled out due to a lack of executive support. Like any initiative that promises dramatic organizational change, a cornerstone of building the Breakthrough IT organization is creating a peer-level relationship between the CEO and CIO, and moving the CIO from a technologist and subject matter expert role to a cross-functional process and strategy expert who can take high-level objectives from the C-suite, distill them into efficient business processes, and facilitate their execution.

Free at Last

The previous chapter delved into the first step in this transition of the CIO's role: eliminating the continuing and utility-based operational aspects of the CIO's daily responsibilities. Gradually transitioning the bulk of the CIO's responsibility from maintaining operations to executing strategy may generate some degree of discomfort for the CIO; what was once a large portion of his or her job responsibility is now in the hands of an independent internal manager, or completely outsourced to another organization altogether. No longer can the CIO hide behind the assumption that just providing services is "good enough." At the same time, the daily battles and operational nuances that robbed time from more valuable efforts have been moved aside, and it is time for the CIO to make the perceptual transition among his or her peers. The first step in this transition is a shift in focus from technology to business process.

Separating Process from Technology

Simply put, a business process takes a series of inputs, performs some action on them, and generates outputs as depicted in Exhibit 3.1. At this basic level, business processes seem quite elementary. Think about

EXHIBIT 3.1

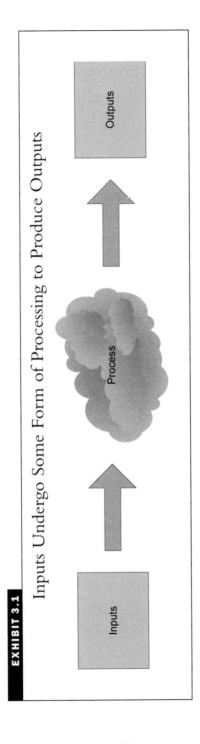

Inputs Undergo Some Form of Processing to Produce Outputs

the process of going to work each morning. Your input is you, in a state of not being at work. Through some process, we end up with the resultant output: you safely arrived at your workplace. While this may seem an overly simple process, it serves to illustrate a point.

When considering the "going to work process," many were probably thinking that "get in the car" should be included in the process, or "take the #2 train." Does the mode of transportation materially affect the outcome of the process? Perhaps the car could break down, or the #2 train could be late on a particular morning, but concerning ourselves with these details puts the focus on a *technology* rather than the process itself. What is critical to the going to work process is not what technology moves the inputs to the outputs, but the fact that we must transport ourselves to the workplace. Think of the process as a generic machine that causes the inputs to change state in order to generate outputs. Water becomes ice through the freezing process, and an understanding of the freezing process does not require one to know whether the water was placed in an icebox, rapidly cooled with liquid nitrogen, or launched into the frigid vacuum of space. When investigating processes, we care only about finding the mechanisms that institute the change of inputs to outputs, not the technologies that facilitate the mechanics of the process.

Content Ain't King

The so-called information revolution has created a surfeit of content. From the billions of web sites to reams of data in a corporate business warehouse, business in general, and more specifically the IT area, has been obsessed with gathering, analyzing, and managing content.

Content is often an input or output to a business process, but when building the Breakthrough IT organization, we must focus on the process and content separately. Think of content as a financial asset. It is certainly important to the ongoing success of the business, but when managing cash, the process of determining how to leverage that cash is more critical than being concerned with whether you are managing euros, dollars, or yuan.

A particular technology is often more closely related to content than it is to process. Vendors have long sold "solutions" that are designed to manage a piece of content in a novel or particular way, serving as a bandage applied to a hemorrhaging process. For example, security solutions have recently come to prominence in the marketplace, each package targeted toward a particular content area: e-mail security, anti-virus software, or detection of hackers or other nefarious forces. A company without a solid threat management process in place may make the mistake of believing that throwing some more technologies at the problem, rather than fixing the underlying process, will prevent any security-related risks to the corporation. After spending money on new technologies and the associated implementation costs, they are left with more technology to create management headaches. These often must be solved at the highest levels of the IT organization as an exception to "standard operating procedure," rather than fixing the underlying threat management process first, and focusing on the technology second.

An ability to separate process from technology and content is an extremely powerful asset in any corporation. Every specialized group within the company generally has a solid grasp on its own particular content area. Human Resources (HR) staff has a strong grasp on the HR field, its issues, and current practices, and the Finance folks generally understand the nuances of corporate finance. What these departments often lack is an understanding of business process. This plays into the hands of the Breakthrough IT organization. IT cannot be expected to be experts on the most esoteric aspects of corporate compliance law, but they can be experts on designing a document management process, perfectly complementing those who do have the detailed compliance knowledge. Similarly, the same personnel who developed a compliance process can work with HR to design a new employee recruitment process. IT's process expertise augments the detailed content knowledge of the rest of the corporation, easily moving from Production to Procurement, and leveraging its knowledge across the corporation without needing to duplicate specific content knowledge.

This shift from content and technology to process knowledge necessitates a shift in IT hiring practices. For too long, IT hiring has been left to HR, who legitimately cannot be expected to be content experts in a particular technology, relying instead on simple and quantifiable benchmarks such as degrees, certifications, or years of experience with a particular technology. Someone with several years of programming experience with the latest application development technology is relatively easy to find, and the presence or lack of some technology certification is as easy to confirm as checking with the certifying agency or asking the candidate to produce some kind of proof. The Breakthrough IT organization requires much more commitment to finding and hiring candidates who are process experts rather than solely technology experts. This process is integral to a successful Breakthrough IT organization if it is to gain and maintain credibility as the "go-to group" within the company, and finding the right employees for the Breakthrough IT organization is covered extensively in the next chapter.

Technology as a Process Enabler

With all this talk of process, one might be wondering where technology fits within the Breakthrough IT organization. The rudimentary ongoing operational processes such as network operations have been outsourced, and now we are talking of abandoning strong technical expertise for process knowledge. How does technology fit into IT as it moves toward Breakthrough status?

In the Breakthrough IT shop, technology serves as a process enabler. As an example, consider generating an invoice to a customer. Whether the invoice is completed by hand on a form, manually typed, or generated from a complex enterprise resource planning (ERP) system, the process remains the same. The invoice must accurately represent the products sold to the customer, contain some basic information about the customer such as name and address, and contain correct calculations related to taxes, shipping, or any appropriate surcharges. The invoicing process should be designed to generate these accurately and efficiently with no errors. Other considerations such as readability and "ease of use" for the customer and features to facilitate rapid payment processing are designed into the process. In this example, selecting which technology should enable the process would involve the following considerations:

Performance. A technical enabler to this process might be able to generate invoices extremely rapidly. For example, an ERP system could generate hundreds of thousands of invoices in an evening versus manually typing a few hundred.

Accuracy. Any business process should have built-in quality checks to minimize errors. A particular technical solution might automate these checks and reference other data or processes to ensure accuracy.

Freeing of valuable resources. Process excellence, combined with appropriate technologies, can lessen the dependency on humans for completing repetitive tasks associated with a process. This aspect of technology selection should be undertaken from a holistic viewpoint, ensuring that any resource savings garnered in one aspect of a process do not create excessive resource requirements to implement or maintain the technology.

Costs. Any technology has an associated cost, and the IT industry has historically done a poor job in predicting, monitoring, and controlling technology implementations based on cost.

In all the preceding cases, it is important to always remember that technology is the "icing on the cake" to a well-designed business process. Despite what vendors may try to sell you, technology in and of itself generally does not impart dramatic business process improvements. Technology should always follow and augment business process; it should not be an afterthought or seen as a cure to ineffective processes.

Where the Rubber Meets the Road: Partnering with the CEO

Much of the content of this book thus far has laid the foundation for building the Breakthrough IT organization, and to this point, many of the concepts and much of the advice can be applied in isolation, bringing gradual improvement to most corporate IT environments. This foundation is certainly not easy to construct. A not-so-subtle shift in thinking is required by the CIO and his or her immediate subordinates; areas of IT's focus once considered critical and a key component of the CIO's "portfolio" have changed their operational sourcing to either an insourced or outsourced model; and management and hiring practices have begun to shift toward a business process focus. Ideally, much of this has been done in partnership or perhaps even at the bidding of the CEO, although much like constructing the foundation of a building, much of the work has happened under the proverbial ground, and out of sight of those outside IT.

Whether the underpinnings of your Breakthrough IT organization exist only conceptually or your IT shop is quickly shedding continuing operations and moving ahead full-steam, an understanding by the CEO of what the CIO is attempting, and what Breakthrough IT means for the corporation as a whole, becomes increasingly critical as you implement the suggestions in this book. Anyone who has spent more than a few months in a corporation, be it large or small, has witnessed the comings and goings of management fads. Heralded with flowery memos and often an onslaught of highly paid consultants, each arrives with fanfare and increasingly confusing titles, conjuring up images of a diet plan or something only an ancient Greek or statistical guru could love. The difference between the management fad that makes for occasional chatter around the water cooler years after it faded from existence, and a new set of ideas and processes that provide true competitive advantage, is often executive support from the top of the organization down.

Like any worthwhile endeavor, building the Breakthrough IT organization is relatively simple in concept: Offload ongoing operations, build a center of business process expertise that functions across the organization, and seek revenue generation by implementing strategic projects. Conceptually, this is as simple as eating less and exercising more to lose weight, yet most entities struggle with both of these simple ideas that require strong commitment to implement. While some organizational changes can be executed in a "guerilla" manner—implemented slowly and methodically without permission or official sanction—a key tenet of the Breakthrough IT organization is a new relationship between the CIO and CEO and the rest of the key executives in the organization. Therefore, buy-in becomes more of a critical issue.

Selling Breakthrough IT

Most CEOs are relative simpletons. *All* they ask is that you generate competitive advantage by outwitting and outfoxing your competitors, all at increasingly lower costs. Breakthrough IT satisfies both requirements, moving IT's source of competitive advantage from being an increasingly lower-cost provider, to providing increasingly valuable process design and implementation expertise across the corporation. This both decreases costs and increases the value that can be generated by IT.

Astute CEOs are also keen to understand and mitigate risk. Perhaps you can recall all the way back to high school physics, and the concept that an object at rest requires a higher amount of force to get it moving than it does to keep it moving. While most CEOs are willing to accept a certain level of risk with existing processes, many require an even more meticulous understanding of the risk inherent in a new tactic before proceeding with its implementation.

In this regard, Breakthrough IT has an advantage in that it is a gradual and steady process. It is not an overnight "business miracle" that requires fanatical commitment and a large assumption of risk, but it does require executive commitment for the long haul, in exchange for spreading the risk of implementing its concepts over a longer period. The biggest risk to implementing Breakthrough IT is the commitment to see it through to fruition. While each successive component of the Breakthrough IT organization provides measurable benefits, the whole is far greater than the sum of its parts.

The first stage in "selling" the idea of Breakthrough IT is to appeal to the criteria mentioned previously, pitching the transition to Breakthrough IT as one that will create a fundamentally different organization than the IT shop of the past, and will likely look different from the IT shop of most competitors. While there is a certain measure of safety in numbers, the simple fact that a traditional utility IT shop often serves as a drag on the organization's bottom line provides a segue into the benefits of Breakthrough IT. Later chapters focus on the delivery of strategic projects as the cornerstone of the return-generating activities of Breakthrough IT. However, in the early stages of remodeling your IT organization, focus on the new manner in which IT will work with the rest of the corporation as it transitions from a technical and engineering focus to a group of business process experts.

The fundamental way in which the IT organization will be serving the rest of the company will change as Breakthrough IT takes hold. This new "engagement model" should be at the forefront of conversations between the CEO and CIO. The Breakthrough IT organization, freed from ongoing utility operations and gradually transitioning to a process focus, will rapidly become irrelevant and fall aside with other management fads if the rest of the corporation, from the CEO down, continues to engage IT using the old model of a shared service center, or technology group to be invoked only when specific technical skills are required. Convincing the CEO of the validity of the Breakthrough IT organization is the first step in changing this perception, but do not assume a single conversation will turn your CEO into a "Breakthrough IT evangelist." The CIO must keep the CEO appraised of the progress in making this transition, just as an interested CEO should continually check in on the CIO and assure the transition to Breakthrough IT status is moving along smoothly, and more importantly, that cost savings and revenue generation delivered by this new style of IT management are actually coming to fruition.

Talking the Talk

The albatross around the neck of any CIO is the perception of the CIO as a technology expert and nothing more, a stereotype nourished by an industry and popular doctrine that suggests a CIO should deliver technical "solutions." Just as word processing software is not a "solution" to the struggles facing a budding novelist, a software or hardware package rarely is more than a set of tools, which will do little to assuage the true strategic and tactical issues facing a business. In the worst of cases, the CIO has little understanding of the company's products, go-to-market strategies, or the threats and opportunities posed by its closest competitors. With the sourcing changes required to begin the successful implementation of Breakthrough IT, the CIO is now free to become a student of his or her own company, assessing the following aspects of the corporation:

- Current markets and industries served by the company, and the different types of customers who inhabit each of these markets.

- Who the key competitors are in each market, and where the corporation places among them. Is it the low-cost, high-volume provider, or a niche player that dominates a very small market?

- Gain an understanding of the top two or three issues facing each market or industry, those that affect the corporation and those that affect customers.

- Learn how the CEO plans to overcome these issues, and where he or she plans to position the company in each of the markets and industries it serves.

This analysis may take several months, and the goal is not to have detailed knowledge of every tiny nuance of the corporation; rather, it is to replace a CIO's technical vocabulary with strategic and tactical parlance, no longer seeing technical "solutions" but being able to share the strategic concerns of corporate leadership, and bring business process expertise to bear that can eventually mitigate those issues. Simply framing future discussions with the CEO and other C-suite colleagues in this manner is the first step in changing the perception of the IT organization.

The goal of IT is no longer to serve as a monolithic organization, providing a service only when summoned, and containing its own bureaucracy that focuses on technology issues rather than helping the other functions of the company solve their business problems. Rather, IT should cross all functions of the company. This should not be confused with building a standard IT organization that is decentralized rather than centrally administered; rather, the Breakthrough IT organization is a centrally managed body that permeates each business function, actively seeking to provide business process design and improvement expertise, rather than just maintaining technologies. Like most successful corporate initiatives, this cross-functional involvement begins at the top of the organization, from the CEO down through the C-suite to line-level managers and employees.

Measuring Success

A successful Breakthrough CIO has moved beyond technology, and his or her new capabilities are recognized throughout the organization. The simple test of success is the CIO's level of involvement in solving a strategic or tactical concern facing the organization. Rarely is a key decision made by the CEO without consulting the CFO to determine the financial impact of a potential change. In addition, any change that might affect the corporation's products or services, or how it markets, sells, or produces those products, likely requires the input of the COO. The true test of determining whether Breakthrough IT is successfully being implemented at your company is whether the CIO is also a key player in these discussions. If the CIO is a valued contributor, helping to analyze the issues and merits of a C-level decision and providing counsel on how to best execute each of the potential options before technology is even mentioned, Breakthrough IT has taken root.

The CEO should also insist that the CIO is evaluated through the lens of value generation and strategy execution. Rather than measuring the CIO through traditional metrics such as budgetary effectiveness and the availability of the systems he or she manages, evaluate where the CIO and the IT organization as a whole have made a measurable and active contribution to other functions within the corporation.

ACTION POINTS

Action points provide concrete steps you can use to begin implementing ideas from this chapter. For this chapter, the action points are:

- Determine the effectiveness of the sourcing changes your organization implemented as described in the previous chapter. Is the CIO truly able to transition from maintaining ongoing operations to his or her new strategic role?

- Assess the talents of the CIO. Is that person aware of the strategic objectives of the company? Is his or her focus shifting from one centered on technology, to a keen understanding and focus on business process?

- Initiate a discussion between the CIO and CEO. This discussion can be triggered by either party, and should demonstrate that:

  - The CIO has a grasp on the challenges and opportunities facing the corporation.

  - The CIO no longer jumps to prescribing a technical solution to every business problem. He or she is shifting focus to actively implementing excellent business processes, and not being called in at the last minute to provide a commodity service.

- The CEO is willing to accept the CIO's new role, and treat the CIO as an agent who can work across different areas of the corporation providing process expertise. The CIO must demonstrate that his or her organization is transitioning to one that is capable of understanding process first and technology second.

- Begin considering how strategic initiatives at the C-level can be positively affected by an IT organization moving toward Breakthrough status. Consider involving the CIO in one of the strategic initiatives the company is embarking on in the near future.

- Develop a new evaluation scheme for the CIO that is focused on his or her transition away from providing a commodity service at a minimum cost to delivering measurable monetary returns.

 Executive Summary

The previous chapter focused on sourcing continuing operational activities to an internal or external provider that could deliver cost savings, and more importantly, remove the operational tasks from the hodgepodge of activities the CIO manages on an ongoing basis. As this sourcing transition occurs, the CIO gains the opportunity to transition his or her focus to helping other C-level executives meet the corporation's strategic objectives. In addition to moving the focus of IT away from continuing operations, the CIO must establish him or herself as a peer of other C-level executives, "talking the talk" on strategy rather than rushing to provide a technical solution to every business problem.

EXECUTIVE SUMMARY (CONTINUED)

The cornerstone of this transition is separating technology from business process. Rather than building an IT organization established on technical expertise, the CIO must change his or her personal focus, and that of the IT organization, to one on process. IT should be able to work with any function of the company, from accounting to shipping, and quickly document, understand, and improve their business processes, applying technology as an augmenter and enabler of the process, rather than as the ultimate solution to a poorly designed or inefficient process.

This is a shift of epic proportions. Typically, IT acted as an independent service provider, delivering a technical solution on an as-needed basis only after being requested by another business unit. IT was often invoked at the last minute, when strategy and process were designed and implemented, and any technical requirements were to be "thrown over the wall" to IT. Changing the mode of engagement between IT and the larger corporation requires a talented CIO, and a CEO who sees the value in the transition to Breakthrough IT. Either party may broach the subject of a transition to Breakthrough IT, but it is critical that the CEO allows the CIO into his or her "inner circle" as the CIO proves his or her worth, and serves as a champion of the transition to Breakthrough status and the evolution of the CIO from a technologist to a businessperson who can provide value through all stages of executing on a particular strategic objective.

Critical to this transition at the C-level is evaluating the CIO based on how effectively he or she is able to execute on strategy, rather than traditional evaluations based on that person's ability to control costs and meet certain service standards. The CIO should also be tasked with tracking the profit and loss on each project undertaken, instituting increased financial rigor within IT in terms of both tracking costs and the monetary returns on each project implemented.

C-Suite Conversations: Greg Buoncontri, CIO of Pitney Bowes

Gregory Buoncontri is vice president and CIO for Pitney Bowes, the world's leading provider of integrated-mail and document-management systems and services. Greg has served in high-level IT positions in several companies, such as Novartis Pharmaceuticals Corporation and ABB and Combustion Engineering, and has worked in IT in a CIO role since 1987.

Like many large companies, Pitney Bowes has seen its share of difficulties and success in implementing large IT projects. When asked why IT fails, Greg indicated that "IT projects fail in a large degree because, one, there isn't an alignment around the target company about what the outcomes are going to be and what is going to be achieved and what has to be done. I think it is very much an alignment issue and a shared vision and a shared agreement—a shared alignment—on the outcome. And the second reason is, in a lot of cases, the organizational structure of the company—and the governance level of the company—is a barrier to it. Talking about, for instance, integration that you get from these big ERP systems so that we can have a common view of the customer—that structure—and you are running the company on a business unit basis; it is not going to work."

Pitney Bowes has several diverse business units, covering everything from financial services to basic mailroom equipment. Aligning all the interests in a portfolio company can be a challenge to the CIO. "Again, the example I am using is, you are looking to integrate and consolidate in a company that has a business unit–centric operating model. What are the chances of two, three, four, seven—however many business units that you have—agreeing on giving programs up, taking things on, if the whole structure of the company is about maximizing what each of those do independently. It is not going to work."

Greg continues, "You have got a portfolio company but you are trying to put in some software and process that is more conducive to some sort of integrated or shared services model. It is going to have a terrible outcome—it will fail. Either it will get implemented badly and the adoption rate will be low or you will spend all the money on it and won't get any of the benefits, and everybody will feel pretty disappointed at the outcome."

This alignment challenge is frequently cited as a failure point for strategic projects. How do you get multiple interests and constituencies to agree to a process that will likely impact their business? Greg feels that this alignment must come from the very top of the organization. "I firmly believe that it is a top-down challenge. The alignment has to start at the very top of the company: 'Where do we want to go?' When you want to depart in a new direction, there are always three big questions: Where are we going, how are we going to get there, and what does it mean to me? Every employee, even if you are the number-two person in the company; the number-one person announces something different that the number-two person also wants to know—if he or she is really honest—what does it mean for me at the end when we get there?" Core to the alignment discussion is the starting vision. For Greg, that is asking, "Where do we want to go?"

Another key to developing business alignment around a process or technology change is who initiates the request for change. Some CIOs see their job as identifying areas where IT can strengthen the business, and then "selling" this change to the respective parties. For Greg, the opposite is true; his ideal scenario is where the business is clamoring for change and the CIO is seen as the person to drive it. Greg notes, "I think you reach a point where it is very hard for any CIO—in fact, maybe close to impossible in some cases—to achieve a push sale. It works best when there is a pull. I would rather have the businesses—my internal customers; the corporate functional heads of the businesses—at my door demanding: 'When are you going to do this for me?' As opposed to me preaching to them: 'Why aren't you doing this?' That is a harder proposition."

When asked about where the IT industry is headed in the coming years, Greg sees several changes in the C-suite. Regarding the state of the CIO role, Greg commented, "I think the current generation of IT leaders has moved beyond being people who are technicians with a CXO title; they are now people who are more business savvy. I think the coming generation will put a different—yet another different—layer of skill on top of that because of the milieu that they are growing up in and their ability to partner with third parties, like outsourcing people to put together coalitions to deliver outcomes. I think that has made the IT person a lot different now than they were 30 years ago when I got into this."

While the core competence of future CIOs may shift from a technical focus to a business process focus, relationships remain a key factor in the CIO's ability to sit at the table with other key executives. "At the end of the day, if you are the world's most brilliant person and let us just say you are running IT but you are incapable of having a good relationship, I don't think it is going to do very much. Now, you could create a relationship and essentially be incompetent—that won't save you either. You have got to have both, but those relationships become very, very important."

The struggle between focusing on continuing operations and executing strategy is a difficult balance, with the Breakthrough IT organization targeting the latter. Greg sees this as an evolutionary process, and one of continual refinement. Greg said, "When I first came here seven years ago and we put the groups together—they were all separate and decentralized and we put them together—I didn't spend any time on strategy. Frankly, I shouldn't have and didn't for a couple of reasons. First, when you put things together and you change the size of the group and change jobs, there is breakage. You have got to fix that breakage. Second, you are usually spending time on that because no one wants to listen to your strategic vision if the day-to-day functionality isn't working right. You have got to be credible." Greg has integrated a phased approach into his work at Pitney Bowes, explaining that, "Stage one is consolidate, make your move, whatever it is. Stage two is to consolidate those gains: Stabilize it, institutionalize it. And then stage three is when you are ready to break through and become that strategic partner." This is not a quick process or panacea, Greg notes. "It might take you five or six years. And then I think it is time to change the model again and you may start the cycle all over again, but you have got to be credible on the basics."

Pitney Bowes seems to be moving in the right direction, with the basics established and operational issues occupying less of the CIO's time. When asked where he sees his own organization in the evolution to Breakthrough IT, he noted: "I think we are well beyond stage two and I think we are in that sort of breakthrough . . . we have got the basics right, and IT is 'How do we use this and what we do' as a platform for expansion of the company. I think we are well positioned to do it."

CHAPTER 4

Clear the Benches
Take Your IT Shop from Dysfunction to Dynamo

A brief walk through the "cubicle city" that is the hallmark of most corporations may reveal a recurring theme: *Dilbert*. The likable and frequently victimized IT wonk suffers through management gaffes, inconclusive meetings, and the latest corporate fads. While certainly good for an occasional laugh, a multitude of *Dilbert* cartoons adorning every cubicle is a sign of trouble. Most people choose their office decorations based on things to which they can relate. Consummate cat lovers have pictures, screensavers, and perhaps even coffee mugs with their feline friends, while motorcyclists have a Ducatti calendar and a helmet stashed under their desk.

While there is nothing wrong with posting a favorite comic on the wall, the frequent *Dilbert* sightings that seem to occur all too often in an

IT department should be cause for concern. If a significant majority of employees see so much of their lives reflected in the comic, and they relate so well to the bespectacled Dilbert and his cohorts that they plaster him all over their cubicles, there is more going on than just having a good laugh.

Many companies with excellent products and solid reputations have faded into irrelevance, either quietly or with headline-making scandals, while a relative unknown with a mediocre product can become an industry dynamo based on a critical factor: the people behind the organization. While both these changes are frequently attributed to brilliant strategies, or the right decision at the right time, at the end of the day, people are making these decisions and people are responsible for their execution.

In *Good to Great*, Malcom Gladwell's landmark study of several companies that went from "respectable" performance to breakaway success, placing them at the top of their industries and the marketplace as a whole, one of the main factors attributed to their excellence was "getting the right people on the bus." Simply put, all the companies in *Good to Great* developed a corporate strategy based on one or two relatively simple objectives—which became the metaphorical "bus." The great companies dismissed anyone who was not prepared to board this bus, and then loaded the empty space with the brightest people they could find, ensuring their goals dovetailed with the direction of the company.

At this point, we have established the high-level objectives of a Breakthrough IT organization: eliminating a focus on utility processes, developing a rapport with C-level colleagues, and transitioning the IT organization's focus from technical and engineering expertise to a group of business process experts. As explained in the preceding chapters, each objective is conceptually quite simple. The bus is moving forward. Now we need to fill it with the right people.

A cornerstone of the Breakthrough IT organization is an organizational transformation from a focus on technical expertise to a focus on business process expertise. This transition is founded in the people who staff your IT organization. If the majority of your staff comes from a technical background, and are hired, trained, and evaluated based on their technical competency, no amount of flowery manifestos from the C-suite nor high-power consultants will be able to shift the focus of your people from technology to process, and transition your organization to Breakthrough status. At the same time, technology has and always will be a core component of an IT organization, and is a highly capable tool for process improvement. While IT staff from the CIO down should be business experts first and foremost, they also require a strong passion for technology.

For the purposes of building a Breakthrough IT organization, "getting the right people on the bus" consists of the following processes:

- Hiring (and firing) the right people
- Continually improving the skills of your people
- Meaningfully evaluating your people

Hiring (and Firing) the Right People

The Top Job: What to Look for in a CIO

The job of the CIO is critical to the success of the Breakthrough IT organization, and he or she sets the tone and guides the transition from an engineering or utility-based organization to a true Breakthrough IT shop. Perhaps the most surprising concept of hiring a CIO is that it should be no different from selecting a COO or CFO, save for that the latter's passions should lie with operations or finance, and the CIO should have a similar level of business acumen, and a passion for technology.

As will be described in the course of this chapter, IT should not be regarded as a unique or outlier organization, compared to Finance or Marketing, for example. Technology is a tool of the Breakthrough IT organization, and any C-level executive who can act in the capacity of a trusted advisor to his or her fellow C-suite executives is an appropriate candidate. A trusted advisor with proven execution capabilities and a passion for technology will make an excellent CIO, even if that passion does not necessarily tie to years of hands-on experience with the technology itself.

Filling the Ranks of the Breakthrough Organization

The origins of most IT shops from an engineering and manufacturing bent continues to trickle down to current HR practices in many companies. All but the most senior positions are delegated to an HR generalist, who applies a simple formula to complete the first-round screening of potential candidates. To make the initial cut, candidates are generally measured against a "punch list" of skills: certifications, degrees, experience with a particular software package or technology, or "pedigree" items such as experience with a particular company or holding a particular title. This punch list is then compared with the "time served" applicable to each item on the punch list, and candidates are then sent on to the next step, or filed in the wastebasket. Candidates are often culled from online resume databases, or if the HR group is slightly more sophisticated, they will hire an agency to sift through online resume databases and make an initial cut before passing those resumes along internally. While this punch list system is reasonably successful at finding technically competent resources, it is difficult to apply such a system to finding appropriate staff for the Breakthrough IT organization.

The punch list model often identifies technically strong candidates, favoring specialists with deep experience in a particular area or technology. As mentioned in previous chapters, this focus on *content* expertise must be replaced with *process* and execution expertise. Rather than hiring an expert in a particular accounting package, we should seek out the person with experience in understanding and modifying accounting processes, and an ability to quickly understand and optimize those processes, either by directly modifying the process or applying technology to improve it. What model, then, is appropriate for finding these types of people?

While occasionally derided as body shops, and known for their high turnover of both grizzled veterans and fresh-faced recent graduates, the top-tier implementation companies such as Accenture, IBM, and the like offer a good example of how to both hire and fire the types of individuals needed in a Breakthrough IT organization. At the entry level, these companies often hire staff with no technical expertise whatsoever, choosing a History major over a Computer Science major based on the former individual's ability to learn, analyze, work in a team, and rapidly understand a new environment. Passion for technology is disconnected from experience with a particular software package or programming toolkit. Employees of the large consulting firms are the quintessential change experts, rarely spending more than a year at any one client site, and then being shipped off to the next assignment, which could be a company in a completely different industry, struggling with a different set of problems.

The bread and butter of these firms is successful execution. Each employee must be able to rapidly get up to speed on a new assignment, and generally work with minimal supervision to drive a series of tasks toward completion.

For experienced hires, the larger implementation firms often look to their competitors' employees for new resources, focusing on pedigree more than certifications or technical expertise. When hiring experienced resources without the pedigree of an esteemed competitor, these companies focus on the candidates' experience working in a project environment. The middle manager, who spent years in a particular position, slowly advancing through the ranks, is often cast aside in favor of a candidate who rapidly moved between different functions in an organization, building a team to execute a fixed-duration project, managing the project to completion or closure, and then disbanding the team and tackling a different challenge.

Letting Go

The large consulting companies also offer a striking lesson in letting people go. Aside from outlier events like sweeping layoffs due to poor economic results or shifts in the industry, the majority of the turnover in the large implementation firms is due to employees leaving. Many are intelligent and qualified people, yet they either do not have enough

passion for the job, or find they simply do not have what it takes. While these firms will certainly do what they can to retain talented people, they do not go through the machinations some other companies engage in to keep an employee. Those who are good at the work and enjoy it stay around as long as they remain interested and continue to perform, while those who lose interest or are underperforming are essentially self-selected out of the organization. These companies are the ultimate meritocracy, highly rewarding top performers and maintaining competitive pressure such that the underperformers or the less passionate quickly depart. If the poor reviews or lackluster raises and bonuses fail to encourage any poor performers who do not self-select out of the company, the employee generally expects the axe will fall soon enough, and the company wastes no time in doing so after one or perhaps two second chances.

Technology and engineering-focused IT organizations have a constant fear of losing "talent": expertise in a narrow niche technology that they perceive as valuable. To combat this possible loss, they will tolerate everything from poor performance to worse interpersonal skills, the whole package being discounted based on a single skill. In the Breakthrough IT organization, each employee must be a jack of many trades, analytical and interpersonal skills being two critical ones. As a company transitions to Breakthrough status, it must have the fortitude to push poor performers to leave the organization, with varying levels of "encouragement" from the company. Excellent performers will demand recognition in the form of advancement opportunities, interesting work, and monetary compensation. Attempts to create the appropriate level of performance will rapidly falter if everyone is recognized and compensated equally.

What to Look for in the Breakthrough Employee

The tired cliché that "the only constant is change" does hold some weight when staffing the Breakthrough IT organization's key members—those who will be implementing the strategic projects that generate measurable cash returns to the business. Often, otherwise good workers struggle in this type of environment. Rather than having years to achieve a deep and all-encompassing understanding of a particular process, staff in a Breakthrough organization will be thrown into unfamiliar territory on a regular basis, with an expected ability to quickly adapt to the new situation, and immediately begin understanding and changing any existing processes.

Exhibit 4.1 highlights some of the differences between the staff of a traditional IT organization, and the criteria to look for in staffing a Breakthrough IT organization.

At its essence, the Breakthrough IT organization needs employees who are:

Analytical thinkers, quickly able to gather and process new information.

Team builders, who can act independently to quickly establish a rapport with new stakeholders, co-workers, and managers, and can create and change the teams of people around various tasks. They are able to both give and take direction from each group. This should not be confused with team players who may be adept at working with others in an existing team environment, but are unable to network, create, and manage teams as needed.

70

EXHIBIT 4.1

HR Process of the Traditional IT Organization versus the Breakthrough IT Organization

.onal IT Organization	Breakthrough IT Organization
on hard skills (technologies, , applications, etc.)	Focus on project experience, independent of the industry or tools implemented
tifications used to qualify ididates' experience	"Pedigree" organizations or highly successful internal projects used to qualify candidates' experience
Jentification of candidates primarily through resume pool keyword searches	Identification of candidates from internal referrals from top-tier employees, recruiting from select schools, and recruiting from leading implementation firms and industry leading firms and competitors
Initial screening process handled primarily through HR	Most of the initial screening process handled by management

Excellent learners, who can independently research a new process, and rapidly gain a basic understanding of new content areas.

Execution-focused employees, who can pick up a new series of goals, measures, and tasks and drive them to completion, successfully managing a project to closure and then rapidly preparing for the next project.

Process experts, who can distill a complex series of interactions into its component steps, and see opportunities for optimization.

Passionate about technology, with a keen interest in learning about and implementing new technologies. This passion need not directly tie to years of experience with technology or active involvement in a technical field. Rather, the candidate should be excited to become a student of technology.

Notice that there is no mention of a particular certification, technology, or software product mentioned. Precisely locating and screening potential employees for the preceding factors is beyond the scope of this book, but an easy starting point is current employees who fit the description of what you are looking for in new hires. Look at their work experience and education and ask them what attributes they feel contribute most to their success. If you find an employee who is able to articulate those skills well, have that person interview potential candidates and seek to identify more people like him- or herself.

Developing requirements for what kind of people you need to advance the goals of your organization is a difficult task in and of itself, yet even more difficult is actually locating these people. While "poaching" employees from large consulting firms or admired competitors is a good option, one resource is often overlooked: those people already on the payroll and their network of colleagues and friends.

The Gold Standard: Referrals

Referrals should form a key component of your hiring practices. If your company is truly an excellent place to work, employees will likely want to share that experience with members of their personal network. Generally, people tend to keep in touch with people who are similar to themselves, so if you encourage your best employees to refer

colleagues, you will likely get more of the same. While referral programs are fairly standard at most corporations, few execute them well. Just as customers referring other customers is a "gold standard" for benchmarking the customer appeal of your goods and services, an employee referral should be given similar value in recruiting new talent.

Each and every referral should be immediately followed up on, preferably by someone who is familiar with the employee who initiated the referral. This person is in a far better position to get an honest assessment of the potential candidate by speaking with the person who made the referral in the first place, and get a far more complete picture of the person than someone in HR glancing at yet another resume that has somehow found its way into the HR mailbox.

Even if there are no current requirements for new employees, contact should be made with the referral and its source, and if nothing else, a quick phone call to the candidate explaining the situation and speaking briefly with the person leaves the door open for future action, and creates a positive impression of your company. Regardless of the current level of job openings, referrals serve another highly beneficial function: They let you truly know if your organization is a place employees enjoy working.

Employee surveys are often seen as the best tool to measure employee engagement, although they are often difficult to design correctly, and involve a small army of survey designers and consultants, statisticians, HR managers, and a mini–marketing campaign to actually get employees to complete the survey. Most employees and consumers alike have also grown suspicious of surveys as an anonymous tool, and despite many assurances to the contrary, most will assume that there is someone looking over their shoulder, often causing them to bias their answers one way or another. As a pure and unadulterated measure of how engaged your employees are, tracking the number of referrals they provide is hard to beat. While many people will answer affirmatively to an anonymous survey when asked if they would buy or recommend a product, few immediately run out and tell everyone they know about the product. In a similar manner, employees may give a company high marks on a supposedly anonymous survey, yet would not wish their current circumstances upon their worst enemy. Tracking employee referrals cuts through all the theory, and is a simple measure of whether your employees actually like their jobs enough to recommend employment to their peers.

Continually Improving the Skills of Your People

Training is one of those funny topics in the corporate world. An entire industry has been built around training, from hiring a "subject matter expert" to deliver a training course to all manner of strange activities, from climbing ropes to building human pyramids, all in the name of learning. While so much energy and money seem to be expended on training, it often seems a distant afterthought during the daily business at hand. Training is one of the first items to be cut from budgets when times are tough, and in heady times, employees are sent to exotic locations to learn skills that will never provide any benefit to the company, save for the fancy certificates that will adorn cubicle walls.

Too often, training is seen as a standalone task, unrelated to an employee's development save for a perception that you need some amount of training every year. Training needs to be a single component to an integrated development plan designed to evaluate the employee, and cultivate and advance that person within the organization. Training must not be perceived as a "gateway" task to acquiring a new skill or assuming a new role. Employees who hesitate to tackle a task with a comment of, "I haven't been trained yet" are not the type of people you want filling the ranks of a Breakthrough IT organization. Most of an employee's learning will come during the course of the job. However, training can provide an introduction to a new skill, or a formal framework, methodology, and vocabulary to an existing skill, serving to crystallize that which has already been practiced in the field.

When evaluating your employees and managers each year, a key component of those evaluations should be a description of the role you see that person developing into in the coming months. From that high-level view, a recipe of job experience, increased responsibilities, and training should be formulated that will help the employee grow into the role you envision.

Be "The Business"

Nothing strikes fear into the heart of the average IT wonk like mention of "The Business," that mercurial group of people that generally represents everyone who is not in IT. "The Business" is often blamed for delayed schedules, or scoffed at for their naiveté when it comes to technical decisions, and similarly, "The Business" blames those in IT for any of its woes even remotely related to technology. Employees of the Breakthrough IT organization must strive to breakdown this distinction between IT and "The Business," and should be hired and evaluated in a manner similar to their peers in Accounting or

Finance. After all, IT is "The Business" as much as any other unit of the corporation.

In addition, the CIO should consider implementing a "tour-of-duty" program, whereby IT staff can spend a defined period of time working in another business unit; similarly, staff outside IT should be given the option to perform a tour of duty within IT. This practice can "cross-pollinate" different competencies throughout the organization; increase the process competence of IT and non-IT personnel, and serve to build better relationships between IT and the rest of the corporation.

Meaningfully Evaluating Your People

Evaluations, both formal and informal, are a critical component of the Breakthrough IT organization. Even if there is no formal "bidirectional" evaluation scheme in place, evaluations are none-theless one of the most significant factors in demonstrating to employees how valuable they are, and how much care you and your organization put into critiquing and facilitating their development. The rushed evaluation, filled with trite comments completed out of duty rather than concern, combined with rewards that have little tie to performance, are a sure way to alienate and sap motivation from employees.

The Breakthrough IT employee described in the previous section is by necessity a feedback junkie, but like any high performer, expects a fair evaluation and rewards for accomplishment, and coaching and guidance in areas of improvement. They will be expected to inde-pendently manage and control projects, and be closely evaluated on the financial outlays and returns associated with each project, with rigorous analysis used to determine the success of the project. This same level of rigor must be applied when evaluating these employees by:

- Establishing performance metrics well in advance of the actual evaluation

- Discussing how to meet those metrics, and any additional skills or resources that might be required to successfully achieve these goals

- Providing periodic reviews with the employee, so any successes can be commended and any shortfalls identified while there is still time to take corrective action

There is no "magic" evaluation methodology that will significantly influence this process, save for ensuring that whatever evaluation system is chosen must provide consistent and frequent feedback, from the CIO down to line-level IT employees. Any successful evaluation process must have both a "goal-setting" component and a "grading" component. The goal-setting component at the highest level asks the question of where the person should be at the next evaluation cycle. This process is often given short shrift, or the person being evaluated is asked to set his or her own goals and objectives, with only a few moments of consideration from his or her manager and a signature constituting this component of the process.

The goals and objectives set the "rules of the game" for each employee, and should provide rigid standards that will be used to measure his or her performance against each objective. They should be set jointly by the employee and manager and discussed, rather than one party dictating them to the other. These goals must be detailed, and any changes in the objectives or measures during the course of the evaluation period should be clearly communicated to the employee and jointly accepted.

There can only be one person in the middle of a performance evaluation. While all may be fair in love and war, a Breakthrough IT shop must conscientiously determine where each employee stands on the performance scale, and reward that person accordingly. The highly competitive and execution-focused employee described in this chapter will have little tolerance for receiving the same ranking as everyone else, both higher and lower performers, and you will cheapen the achievements of the top employees by attempting to institute a bell curve in a misguided notion of playground-style fairness.

 ACTION POINTS

Action points provide concrete steps you can use to begin implementing ideas from this chapter. For this chapter, the action points are:

- Evaluate the CIO, or if you are the CIO of an organization, perform a self-evaluation. Is the CIO a trusted advisor of other C-level executives? Is he or she a competent businessperson with a proven track record of execution and a passion for technology? Does he or she select highly talented individuals to fill the ranks of the IT organization, looking for these same characteristics in each employee?

- Study the hiring policies of your IT organization, and if they are an HR-based activity that is focused on hiring candidates using a "punch list" of technical criteria, institute a shift toward evaluating candidates based on business acumen and project experience.

- Ensure that any referral programs that are in place put referrals by top performers into the top of the hiring pipeline, quickly contact the referred candidate, thank the employee for the referral, and keep that person updated on the hiring process.

- Focus hiring efforts on several high-quality educational institutions, or look to "marquee" firms and competitors known for their top talent, rather than scouring resume pools.

- Bring rigor to your employee evaluation process, taking the time to jointly set goals and objectives each evaluation period, explaining how to meet those goals and how the employee will be measured against them. Employees are the core of the organization, and this process must not be treated as more paperwork to be ignored and disposed of in the least painful manner.

- Integrate training into the evaluation process, selecting training programs that augment each employee's work experience, and help each person move to higher levels of the organization.

- Consider a "tour of duty" whereby IT employees spend time in a business function, and vice versa. This will expand the experience levels of each group, and serve to break down the walls between IT and "The Business."

- When evaluating employees, remove superficial attempts at "fairness" and the temptation to rank all employees in the middle of the scale to prevent conflict. High performers demand to know where they stand, and will quickly see through attempts at skewing rankings in the name of fairness.

EXECUTIVE SUMMARY

Like every other component of a modern corporation, the people who fill the various functions and roles often dictate the success or failure of the company. The CIO defines the makeup of the Breakthrough IT organization and, like any other C-level executive, he or she should have a strong business focus in addition to a passion for technology. This executive should be able to fill the role of trusted advisor to the other C-suite executives, and staff his or her IT organization with employees who have a similar focus on business process, successful execution, and a passion for technology.

Employees of the Breakthrough IT organization should not follow the traditional paradigm that originates in engineering and manufacturing organizations, whereby employees are selected primarily based on their technical skills and years of experience with a particular tool or technology. Rather, employees should have a track record of successfully executing projects in a dynamic work environment, such as that of a large implementation firm. The presence or absence of a particular technical tool on their resume should be ignored, and business experience and an ability to quickly understand and modify business processes the preferred benchmark of their experience.

These employees should be carefully sought, with IT driving the selection process rather than HR culling from online resume pools. Current employees in other business units, and referrals from high-performing employees, should be the preferred source of qualified candidates, and a group of select educational institutions and marquee firms known for developing excellent employees should be selected as a source of new talent.

Training and evaluating are key components of retaining high-caliber employees within the Breakthrough IT organization. Training should be aligned with the evaluation process, and serve as an enhancement and augmentation to the employee's skill set, rather than a one-time event that does not help the employee develop to the next level of success. Evaluations must be honest, and feedback on positive achievements and coaching and areas for improvement must go hand in hand. Breakthrough IT employees are expected to be high performers, and the evaluation process must honestly rank each employee and recognize and reward the highest performers. There is no room for "fairness" in the Breakthrough organization, as nothing will sap the will of the highest performers as quickly as being ranked in the middle to avoid hurting the feelings of lower performers.

CHAPTER 5

Milking the Cow
Turn Your IT Project Portfolio into a Cash Cow

"Tweaking our portfolio should not take too long this year," explained Marissa, the CIO of Breakthrough Corp. "I think our allocation was just about right last year."

"The market seems on the cusp of a slowdown, so I don't want to get too aggressive. I think we really need to pull back on our riskiest investments," observed Jim, Marissa's boss and CEO of the company.

"I've seen the same signs. I've prepared a draft allocation model that I'd like to spend some time on. I'm going to review it with the Program Office next week as we determine which strategic projects to pursue next year." Marissa pulled out her allocation model—not of a traditional investment portfolio, but rather, detailing the different classes of projects Breakthrough Corp would be investing in, each ranked according to risk, the expected ROI of each, and the timeframe to achieve that ROI. It also spelled out past returns for each project class, carefully tracked since Marissa spearheaded the company's transition to a Breakthrough IT organization.

The preceding chapters laid the foundation for the Breakthrough IT organization, sourcing ongoing operations to reduce their cost and "mindshare," building support for Breakthrough IT in the C-suite, and transitioning IT staff from technical experts to process and business experts with a passion for technology. While these changes may have shaken your IT organization to its core, they are just the first step in creating a Breakthrough IT organization, and have focused on setting the stage for the return-generating aspect of Breakthrough IT: implementing strategic projects.

Perhaps more than any other unit in the corporation, IT has long had a project focus. Whether rolling out the latest desktop operating system or delivering a multiyear implementation of the latest CRM package, the exciting days and long nights celebrated and lamented by IT executives are often due to project implementations. This project culture has imbued IT with several unique characteristics, from the obvious such as project management talent, to subtle relationships and experience working with every business unit and function within the corporation.

At the same time, these projects are often approached with trepidation by both IT and business leadership, memories of the latest large-scale project failure fresh in their minds from the business press, or perhaps a stingingly painful implementation within their own company. Perhaps that project was one that took far longer than expected, cost multiples more than the original budget, and delivered a fraction of the value that was promised in the early days of formulating the business case.

So, what is needed to both assuage the legitimate concerns of costly failure and contribute to a higher likelihood of success? The odds have been stacked in our favor by transitioning ongoing operations, and swelling the IT ranks with process experts. To begin the implementation of successful strategic projects, we must start by building formality into their selection, execution, and monitoring, and regarding all projects within the organization as part of a unified portfolio. Similar to an investment portfolio, the project portfolio allocates a portion of available funds to investments with a particular risk profile. If we were at the end of our working career and considering retirement investments, we would generally stick to safe investments, trading lower risk for significantly lower returns, as opposed to someone at the beginning of his or her working life, with a high appetite for risk. Similarly, a company in a mature market, with stockholders demanding stable returns, would have a very different project portfolio than a company making maverick decisions in the hopes of expanding market share or outwitting a competitor.

Developing a Project Investment Mix

Before the detailed work of creating a formal governance structure and beginning to assess an organization's project portfolio, an investment mix should be formulated that will guide project decisions from the top down. This decision should be made with the care and somberness of any other investment decision, due to concern with the sheer amount of money spent on organizational projects, and because the right investment mix and successful execution are the

EXHIBIT 5.1

The Risk/Return Matrix for Project Portfolio Analysis

Allocation	Risk	Return Timeframe	Description
30%	Low	Short	Quick fix
		Medium	
		Long	Infrastructure and maintenance
60%	Medium	Short	"Bread and butter" projects:
		Medium	process fixes, new tools, etc.
		Long	Foundational (ERP, CRM, etc.)
10%	High	Short	Reactionary
		Medium	Experimental
		Long	R&D

backbone of Breakthrough IT. All other things being equal, two similar IT organizations at different companies will gain or lose competitive advantage based on how they chose an investment mix for their IT project spending.

Like any other investment, two basic factors drive the development of a project investment mix: risk and timing of return on investment. Exhibit 5.1 details the combinations of risk and return horizon, providing a recommendation as to which classes of project fit within each combination.

At a basic level, the percentage of your organization's project budget allocated to each risk category should be designed to dovetail with the rest of the company's strategic objectives. If a market has stagnated and the company is hoarding cash to prevent a crisis, IT investment should tend toward lower risk projects. If the rest of the company is executing a maverick growth strategy, IT should target medium-risk foundational projects, and higher-risk experimental and R&D projects, in an attempt to gain an edge in a rapidly changing market.

The percentage of your project budget spent in each category is a key factor in developing your investment mix, and it is critical to ensure that you minimize the number of projects that have a risk-and-return horizon combination well outside their class. For example, if a proposed infrastructure project has an extremely high risk and a long return horizon, it should be regarded with strong suspicion. One would not consider investing in a financial instrument with a 1 percent return over a 10-year period, with a 99 percent chance of losing the entirety of the initial investment, any more than one would consider an extremely risky hardware upgrade with a very long return horizon. Similar analogies to investing can be also used for projects that sound too good to be true. Projects that promise huge overnight returns with little or no risk are rarely the opportunity of a lifetime, and more likely an empty promise that will result in vanished funds.

The PASRBRTKO: Project Analyzing, Selecting, Risk-assessing, Budgeting, Returns Tracking, and Killing Office

The Project (or Program) Management Office (PMO) has unjustly received a bit of a bad name. Like the selling of "solutions" that were really technologies looking for a problem, PMOs were touted as the answer to any failed project, and a silver-bullet solution for organizations that struggled with successfully implementing projects. Like good software pasted over a horribly dysfunctional business process, throwing some IT folks in a room and calling it a PMO rarely helped these struggling organizations. A PMO must be more than the name of yet another administrative bottleneck. An effective PMO is the initiator and monitor, and is ultimately responsible for the completion of all projects, and captures and disseminates the organization's project knowledge for future use.

The other key to an effective PMO is that it is not strictly an IT initiative. Key PMO decisions, especially those around beginning, extending, or suspending a project, cannot be made in isolation of the business units they affect, and bringing in decision makers from other business units only during trying times engenders a poor decision-making process. The PMO represents a governing body for the organization's projects, and as such, must be composed of representatives from each component of the company.

The PMO covers three primary roles in managing the organization's projects:

1. Auditioning and initiating

2. Monitoring and controlling

3. Closing and capturing knowledge

Auditioning and Initiating Projects

One of the central roles of the PMO is to create a defined process in which projects are submitted, reviewed, and analyzed for their fit within the organization's project portfolio, and then initiated or shelved. An organization that manages this process poorly is like an undisciplined investor, pouring his or her money into the latest "flavor of the month" stock or mutual fund, and overweighting and underweighting particular investment classes due to that investor's lack of a cohesive strategy. In a strong market, these investors can do well despite themselves, just as organizations with no real strategy to their project allocation model can conceal the absence of a defined strategy due to economic conditions or repeated heroic efforts by their implementation teams.

With a defined project investment mix in place, a nominating committee and an associated process should be developed, one that can weed out poorly conceived projects while providing a forum that does not throw up so many roadblocks as to encourage each business unit to execute its own clandestine projects. There should be little magic to the submission process, and a simple idea should be all that is required to gain the PMO's attention and consideration for a project. A series of gates can be established, each requiring more information from the requestor than the previous, until the project gains enough momentum that returns can be estimated and a rough timeframe plotted. At this point, the potential project should be presented to a final selection committee.

The two most important things about this committee are:

1. Voting members are defined and universally known well in advance. Anyone may lobby or provide comment, but only a defined group has a yes or no vote, which is *never* subject to second guesses. The CEO and CIO should hold a position on this selection committee: its makeup may change slightly depending on the project under consideration, but the final decision must be respected at all levels of the organization.

2. A decision to move forward is final, unless dire circumstances necessitate reconsideration. Nothing saps organizational will like a constant second-guessing of major decisions.

While this decision-making process may sound ruthless, a transparent process that is not subject to backroom dealing, or massive voting sessions and endless meetings peppered with the corporate equivalent of a filibuster, will command respect across the organization.

In addition to a defined group of decision makers and a transparent process, each potential project should be subjected to the same level of analysis. This standardized process allows for projects with different outcomes, methodologies, targets, or any combination thereof to be compared on a relative basis. Most organizations have a defined and complex method for evaluating projects, and while many elements of an existing process can and should be reused as the organization moves to Breakthrough status, they should drive toward answering two simple questions: What is the expected ROI for the project, and what is the timeline for that return?

As explained earlier in the chapter, the project portfolio should include projects at various levels of risk, covering short-, medium-, and long-term return horizons. Determining the expected return and the timeline to recoup that return allows the project selection committee to look at each potential project as a standalone activity, and as it relates to the rest of the project portfolio. Even if a project looks appealing when considered on its unique merits, the organization as a whole may be overloaded in one particular dimension of the risk/return horizon matrix, and should either curtail other projects in that area of the matrix or pass on the project under consideration.

Like the project selection committee, whatever methods are used to determine ROI and return horizon must be applied consistently and transparently, and should be determined by a cross-functional group.

IT traditionally is not well regarded for its ability to accurately predict ROI, so involvement from corporate finance lends credibility to the predictions for each project and provides additional expertise.

Red Light

Once ROI and the return horizon for a project have been calculated by a cross-functional team, the project analyzed on its unique merits, a determination made as to how it fits into the organization's project portfolio, and the case presented to the project selection committee for a vote, it is time to start the project or shelve it for future consideration. The easier process, shelving the project, is often done the most poorly. Certain factions within the organization may continue to lobby for the project, wasting the time of the PMO and selection committee, or the analysis and business case for the project may simply be lost in the zeal to move on to the next activity. It is the responsibility of the PMO to ensure neither of these fates befalls a rejected project.

All the analysis that was done for the project should be captured in a central repository, from something as simple as a three-ring binder to an advanced content management solution. More critically than the way the documents are stored is a process to review the project on a defined schedule and "reactivate" the project for consideration with a minimum of time spent redoing old work. A summary of the benefits and drawbacks of the project, reasons for rejecting it from considera-tion, and "stumbling blocks," or problems and circumstances that prevented the project from moving forward, should be recorded. A future date should also be set to review the project if any of the stumbling blocks were due to time-related factors. For example, if a project was rejected due to budgetary concerns, or the organization's project portfolio was too heavily loaded in a similar area, a date should be chosen when the project will be reconsidered to determine whether the stumbling block still exists.

Even projects the organization would likely never attempt and that are unanimously rejected should at least receive a cursory review once a year. Market conditions may have changed, or the analysis that was done on even the most foolhardy effort may contribute to a more lucrative project in the future.

Green Light

After the proverbial dust has settled and all votes have been tallied, a project that has been given the green light requires careful planning on the part of the PMO before the work of delivering the project begins in full swing. Organizations often go through the tedium of analyzing and carefully developing a business case for a project, give it the green light, and then promptly "forget" all the work that was done before the project began, letting the business case and risk analysis sit in a binder on someone's shelf, sentenced to a life of collecting dust. While the temptation is strong to immediately form a team and start executing the project, the PMO should ensure that:

- The business case is summarized, and key points and metrics from the business case are captured in an easily accessible and widely distributed format. If a project begins to struggle, evaluating its current state against the original business case can prove invaluable.

- The same should be done with any risk assessments that were performed. The project can be assessed against these risks on a regular basis, which can serve as an early warning sign that the project is in danger.

- Any analyses of the internal or external business environment should be retained and reviewed on a regular basis. If the project was given the green light based on certain assumptions about the business environment, care should be taken to monitor these external factors, and if they change, modify the project or cancel it if there are risks of it becoming irrelevant.

The PMO should establish a reporting framework based on the analysis that was conducted, both in an effort to provide an initial set of high-level criteria for monitoring the project, and to constantly perform a "sanity check" and verify that the project is delivering on its expected returns while staying within its cost and resource constraints. It is also helpful to determine "drop-dead" figures on minimal returns and maximum resource consumption before starting to execute the project. Rather than spending sleepless nights wondering if just a few more bodies or a few more dollars will save the project, spending and return ceilings take away the guesswork and put a stake in the ground before the project is in full swing.

With high-level metrics in place, and returns and risks captured and distributed to form the basis of detailed project monitoring, the PMO is almost ready to hand the execution of the project off to a project manager or group of project managers to perform the day-to-day delivery of the project. Before the handoff, the PMO should complete the following tasks to ensure the project manager can rapidly begin the work of delivery:

- Form a stakeholder committee with representatives from the PMO and the business units that will be affected by the project. Depending on the size and scope of the project, there may be several subcommittees, but like the project selection committee, the ultimate group of voting stakeholders should be defined and known in advance. This group will have the power to decide on scope changes, or changes to the original business case, and in many cases recommend or deny requests for additional funding or resources.

- Provide a list of key contacts within the business units that are relevant to the project. As most of these people actively participated in the project selection process, they should be known to the PMO, and providing them to project managers in advance will save work in the discovery phase of the project.

- Deliver a repository of standard tools and templates to the project manager. Your organization may enforce varying levels of compliance to the corporate documentation standards, but if nothing else, providing tools and templates from other projects spares the implementation team from wasting time recreating documentation, and ensures some level of standardization among the organization's projects.

When this handoff is complete, the PMO has less active responsibility for the project than it did during the selection process. However, it should be the key body for monitoring the high-level status of the project, and ensuring that the project continues to positively contribute to the organization's project portfolio.

Monitoring and Controlling Projects

The detailed monitoring of a project should be based on the portion of financial returns it has generated as the project is delivered. This monitoring is covered in detail in the next chapter, but the PMO's responsibility in monitoring ongoing projects should not be overlooked. Rather than monitoring projects at a detailed level, focused on the tasks or deliverables that have been completed by the project team, the PMO should monitor the return that has been delivered by the project. Each major project component should be broken out, and given a specific monetary return and the timeframe required to achieve that return. The PMO can then look at each project much like an investor, determining if the returns are acceptable based on current internal and external conditions. Regardless of how much effort or money has been spent on a project, the basic question at the PMO level should always be whether the money and resources could be better spent elsewhere. This is a complex decision, but provides an appropriate framework for looking at individual projects as part of the overall project portfolio, and helps avoid situations where "just a bit more" money or resources are constantly being diverted to a struggling project when those resources could generate more impressive returns by contributing to another effort.

The other critical task of monitoring projects at this high level is ensuring that any dependencies between other projects are appropriately tracked and managed. If a particular project lays the technical or organizational foundation for a series of other projects, it must be closely monitored, and other projects either pushed forward or throttled back depending on the status of the foundation project.

Many companies prefer to separate organizational or process change projects from technical projects, in which case the PMO's role as a coordinator between projects becomes even more difficult and critical.

Closing and Capturing Knowledge

Ending a project is often one of the most difficult tasks an organization faces. In the case of a project that is terminated before achieving its objectives, there is a rush to disassociate with the failed project and bury the proverbial dead before they start to stink. With a successful project, there are rounds of parties and promotions, with most of the people who engendered the project's success seeking to capitalize on that success and parlay it into higher positions in the organization, wherever those positions may be found. In either case, consultants and vendors are loathe to stay on a project where the end is in sight, and even if they remain on the project team, much of their focus is on finding the next project before they are no longer required.

The rush to move away from failure or cash in on success while the memories of victory are still fresh in everyone's mind is expected, and while it cannot be completely avoided, the PMO should plan and monitor the closure of the project and ensure:

- Any detailed knowledge about the project is captured, organized, and archived in a readily accessible format. This is often expected in technical projects in which reams of esoteric development documentation are stored, but process documentation, benchmarks, and organizational diagrams should all be captured in case the project is ever revisited, expanded, or applied to other parts of the corporation. This work can also provide a starting point for other projects, generating some benefit from even an otherwise failed project.

- The project has transitioned from a fixed duration endeavor and has become "operationalized," with a support team and standard processes and procedures in place. Well before the official close of the project, this transition should begin, and the business units that were affected by the project should be able to function without the ongoing aid of the original project team.

"Knowledge transfer" is often touted by the implementation firms, yet rarely occurs in their zeal to move their people to the next project before they are no longer needed. A savvy PMO will treat this activity as seriously as any other task or deliverable, and ensure the appropriate people in the corporation are trained and self-sufficient. A formal review and signoff are appropriate and encouraged.

Whether the project failed completely or was a rousing success, each person on the project team should be evaluated independent of the mitigating circumstances, and high performers should be appropriately rewarded and staffed on another project or back in an operational role. Avoid the urge to punish the entire team for a project's failure. As the PMO is aware of the entire organization's project portfolio, this review is an ideal time to scout for new talent that can aid other projects within the corporation.

Closing a project is a project in and of itself, and an area the PMO should drive. Developing standard checklists and procedures allows the PMO to track the previous points, allowing the project team to remain focused on the tasks at hand. The PMO must act in a highly visible and evenhanded manner, assuring the staff on the project that there are roles in the organization when the project closes, and that their tour of duty on a project team will not put them at a disadvantage to their peers who remained in operational roles.

In effect, the PMO serves as the steward of the project portfolio, monitoring results and changing investments as appropriate with the CEO, CIO, and CFO as the ultimate clients of the PMO. The PMO also provides standard toolkits and knowledge that can be applied to each of the projects in the organization, and works with HR to ensure that project staffs are provided operational roles or a slot on another project team once their current project completes. While the concept of a PMO initially seems like one more layer of organizational bureaucracy, it is more like a liaison from one project to another, and from a project to the rest of the organization as depicted in Exhibit 5.2.

Note that the role of the PMO includes an operational component to capture and disseminate knowledge, provide logistical support, and interact with other business units, and also includes a strategic aspect that interacts directly with the C-level executives of the corporation. The overall goal of these two roles is to ensure the project portfolio continues to deliver optimum returns to the company.

What the PMO Is *Not*

One of the biggest risks with implementing a PMO structure within an organization is the creation of another layer of bureaucracy. A poorly run PMO can become a self-serving beast, demanding increasing amounts of data from projects, clogging calendars with status meetings, and creating rigid rules that take hours to understand and comply with.

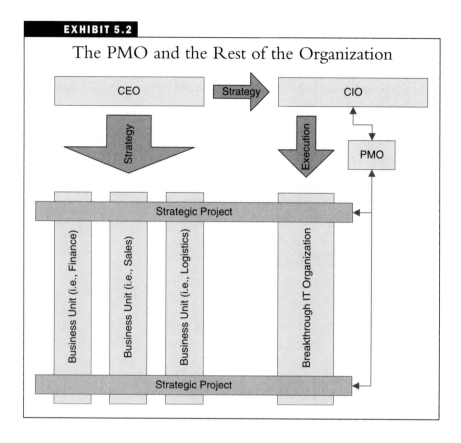

EXHIBIT 5.2

The PMO and the Rest of the Organization

The PMO is not a reporting or rulemaking body at its core; rather, the primary objective of the PMO should always be to facilitate the execution of individual strategic projects, and consolidate information about each for management reporting and project portfolio analysis purposes.

While standardized toolkits and predefined materials are an excellent way to speed up the initial phases of a project, the PMO should not be so rigid as to demand every single project stick within its guidelines. Just as a carpenter would be foolish to use a hammer for every woodworking task, the PMO should not be allowed to become so unwieldy as to assume a single tool is applicable to every situation and every project.

Representatives from the C-suite should frequently seek feedback on the success of the PMO from individual project teams, both those that are successful and those that failed. Like any group within the organization, the PMO should never be exempt from improving its own processes, or allowed to grow to the point where it becomes a self-serving layer of administrative overhead.

 ACTION POINTS

Action points provide concrete steps you can use to begin implementing ideas from this chapter. For this chapter, the action points are:

- Examine your current project selection process. Is it rife with backroom dealings and decisions made behind closed doors? Can anyone and everyone within the organization derail the voting process, demanding consideration at the expense of an efficient and transparent selection process?

- Evaluate your project portfolio and determine the ROI and the return horizon for each project. Is your company over- or underweighted in a particular area? Are you spending too much time and money on high-risk projects, or continually sticking with low-return, low-risk projects?

- Examine completed projects, both those that were highly successful and those that were dramatic failures. Capture lessons learned and best practices from each to form an organizational body of knowledge that can be maintained and disseminated by the PMO.

- Examine your current PMO or equivalent. Does it serve both a strategic and operational role, or is it more of an administrative function? Develop an action plan to transition your current PMO to the Breakthrough IT model.

- Transition the PMO's current status reporting to one based on each project's current ROI, and how it is performing in relation to other projects in the portfolio. This reporting should be used at the highest levels of the organization to determine which projects to continue funding, and serve as an early warning mechanism for determining which projects may be in trouble.

- Ensure the PMO is serving as a communication broker among other projects, business units, and human resources. The PMO should provide coordination and logistical support to each individual project, and monitor the dependencies and interactions between projects.

 EXECUTIVE SUMMARY

The key element of the Breakthrough IT organization is that it generates measurable value for a corporation. The primary means to that end is through the successful execution of projects that help an organization execute its business strategy. Rather than being managed as isolated entities, projects should be evaluated in the context of a project portfolio. Much like an investment portfolio, the project portfolio seeks to have an appropriate balance of high- and low-risk projects that have a mix of return horizons, from short to long.

Each individual project is evaluated in terms of how it will contribute to delivering an element of the organization's strategy, and how it fits within the current project portfolio. There may be excellent

Executive Summary (continued)

potential projects that should be rejected since they are inappropriate in the context of the larger project portfolio.

The internal organization responsible for the evaluation, selection, and monitoring of projects is the centralized Program (or Project) Management Office (PMO). The PMO ensures projects are evaluated based on their fit within the project portfolio, and establishes a voting mechanism for the final selection of a project. Only a select group well known to the organization at large should have a vote in selecting projects. Lobbying and presenting various aspects of the business case to those with a vote is acceptable, but giving too many people a vote is counterproductive.

The PMO is also tasked with initiating the project should it be given an affirmative decision, or documenting the current business environment that led to rejection of the project should the decision be revisited as the environment changes. After initiating, the PMO continually monitors the project, reporting on its status in the context of the overall project portfolio to the CEO, CIO, and CFO. If a project begins to stumble, it is evaluated like any other investment; if returns are not adequate, the money is reallocated to another venture.

The PMO should be tasked with closing projects, whether they are successful or a dramatic failure. In either case, useful knowledge can be captured, and several star performers identified who should be redeployed regardless of the outcome of the project. It is important to note that the PMO plays a strategic role in managing the organization's project portfolio and selecting projects and an operational role in providing support to each project, and serves as a liaison between projects. The essence of the PMO is both a facilitator and broker of knowledge and connections between other projects and business units. It should not merely be another layer of bureaucracy.

CHAPTER 6

Show Me the Money
Controlling a Project by the Numbers

W e live in a management culture obsessed with numerical data. Management dashboards, advanced statistical analysis, and complex customer surveys feed the drive to "manage by the numbers." While the transition away from business decision making based on gut feel and intuition has largely been helpful, we are nearing a numerical crisis. Statistical and numerical analyses drive business decisions without the decision maker fully understanding the components of that number. An even more insidious trend is that the demand for numerical data, coupled with its building complexity, has allowed many "gut feel" predictions to masquerade as hard data, through trendy buzzwords and complex-looking presentations with little solid data behind them.

Imagine a meeting with the CFO of a large organization. His minions gather around a polished oak boardroom table, the seats filled with women and men in crisp business attire. The lights dim, a projector whirs to life, and the manager du jour glosses over a few introductory slides. Finally, the "meat" of the presentation flashes onto the screen. The grizzled CFO glares at each person in turn, asking for the current financial health of the corporation.

"Well," quips the first victim, "I've checked with each of the area managers, and as you can see on the slide, they all report a "green" status.

"What does profitability of the new product line look like?" asks the CFO, barely looking away from the dazzling sea of green boxes on the slide.

"That's a green light as well. You might notice that our 'waste removal' area manager reports an increase in costs for garbage removal from the executive suites, so we've reported that as a yellow light."

"Excellent work" mumbles the CFO, turning toward the seat to the left. "Are our profit numbers still green? I've got the analyst call later this afternoon and I'm hoping for good news."

Anyone who has ever spent time in the financial organization of a company is likely cringing after reading that story. The thought of an organization reporting data as crucial as earnings and expenses to the CFO of the organization with a three-color system of charts and fancy graphs with no supporting evidence behind the numbers would send investors running to the phones to dump stock in such a company, and mobilize armies of auditors and regulatory bodies. While this situation sounds comically far-fetched, a similar scene takes place in the offices of the IT department in most organizations, large and small.

IT is presumed to have a certain technical sophistication versus the rest of the organization, and as the keeper of the data is expected to have a wealth of information to analyze and use to support decision-making processes. A stroll through most IT departments certainly would imply that they are at the top of their management game. Large charts or animated screens show various graphs and numbers, often accompanied by impressive "red light/green light" charts covering multiple areas of data, as if the abundance of different chart formats and colors will bring about "death by numbers" and numb the viewer into forgoing any questions on whether the department is actually performing well. The unfortunate subtext to this numerical assault is that it usually works.

Exhibit 6.1 pictures one such chart, similar to one used in an actual meeting of the CEO, CIO, and other key executives for a large company implementing an ERP system.

Similar to the hypothetical story at the beginning of the chapter, this chart was used to present a detailed view of the health of the project. Snappy graphics and abundant text gave an air of analytical validity to the chart; however, determining the actual green, yellow, or red status for each area was merely a matter of asking area managers for their opinion on the status of the project. Despite its impressive colors, this chart carries no more hard data or value than bringing in each manager and asking, "Well, how do you *feel* about the world today?"

Despite all the green lights, the project eventually missed two go-live dates, took twice as much time to implement versus what was originally planned, and required nearly three times the original budget.

EXHIBIT 6.1

Risk Management Scorecard

Area of Focus	Sales	Prof Svcs	Tech Supp	Mktg	P2P	OTC/Comm	HR	MTB
Cutover								
Project								
1 Are you fully engaged in the cutover process?	Y	G	G	G	G	G	G	G
2 Are you aware of any project cutover issues that give you serious concern?	G	G	G	G	G	Y	G	G
3 Is your organization prepared to validate data as required by the cutover plan?	G	G	G	G	G	G	G	G
Internal Users								
4 Are you aware of any cutover issues related to your internal customers that give you serious concern?	G	Y	G	G	Y	G	G	G
External Users								
5 Are you aware of any cutover issues related to your external customers that give you serious concern?	Y	Y	G	G	G	G	N/A	G
Cutover Issues/Risks								
6 Are you aware of the details of the cutover plan and have you committed the required resources to its execution?	G	Y	Y	G	G	G	G	G
7 Are you aware of the process transition and cut-off plan between 4/1 and 4/24? Systems Process Data	G	Y	Y	G	G	Y	G	Y
Master Data for Go Live								
8 Have you dedicated sufficient resources to the execution and validation of the master data and transactional data conversion plans?	Y	Y	Y	G	G	G	G	Y
9 Are you comfortable that the Master Data Organization can support your business area?	Y	Y	Y	G	Y		G	
Business Readiness								
Organizational Alignment								
10 Do you feel that your organization is structured to effectively support all business activities after go live?	Y	G	Y	G	G	Y	Y	G
11 Do you have regular meetings with your SPOC/Workstream Lead to review status and resolve issues?	G	G	G	G	G	G	G	G
12 Have you reviewed the organizational impact document and taken necessary steps to communicate changes that will be impacting your area of the business?	G	G	Y	G	G	G	G	Y
Organizational Role Mapping								
13 Have you reviewed the role-mapping for your business area?	G	G	Y	G	G	Y	G	G
14 Are you satisfied that role-mapping that has been done will enable efficient and effective process operation in your business area?	G	Y	Y	G	G	Y	G	G
Communications								
15 Have you defined all appropriate communication needs, for both internal and external impacted audiences, and worked and provided a schedule for execution to the Business Readiness Communications Team?	Y	Y	Y	G	G	G	Y	Y
Training & Performance Support								
16 Have you reviewed the training curriculum and materials, and are you confident that the training will adequately prepare your business?	G	Y	Y	G	Y	G	G	G
17 Have you reviewed the training schedule and committed any works team resources to its delivery, where appropriate?	Y		Y	G	G	G	G	Y
18 Is management within your business area aligned with the required training delivery plan.	Y		Y	G	G	G	G	Y
IT Readiness								
19 Have you reviewed and are you comfortable with the plans relating to the following: Desktop Readiness Printer Readiness	G	Y	Y	Y	G	G	G	Y
Site Readiness & Go Live Support								
20 Are you aware of how customer inquiries will be handled through the Customer Care "1-800" number?	G	Y	G	G	G	G	N/A	N/A
21 Are you aware of and aligned with your role in post go live customer support?	Y	G	Y	G	N/A	G	Y	Y
22 Are you aware of your role in supporting your CBPO?	G	G	G	G	G	G	G	G
23 Do you have regularly scheduled meetings with your CBPO to stay aligned with their needs and expectations regarding project outcomes and go live?	G	G	G	G	G	G	G	G
24 Are you aware of the post go-live "Super user" plan and have you committed sufficient resources (i.e., "Super Users") to its execution?	G	Y	G	G	Y	G	Y	G
Process Readiness								
25 Does your process area have robust and credible plans to ensure that all April business is entered into SAP between 4/25 and 4/30 (including any related staffing needs).	Y	Y	G	G	G	G	Y	G
26 Have you reviewed the SOX process documentation and scheduled a process walkthrough leading to its approval?	G	Y	Y	N/A	Y	Y	Y	Y
27 Have process walkthroughs and/or system demos (including contingency plans) been scheduled for your area of the business?	G	G		G	G	G	Y	G
Business Readiness Issues/Risks								
28 Have you defined a contingency plan to resolve potential issues at go live?	G	G	Y	Y	Y	Y	Y	
Business Related Testing								
UAT		G	G					
29 Can you support UAT based on the current schedule?	G	G	Y	G	G	G	Y	Y

The Right Stuff: Determining What to Measure

When it comes to enterprise projects, one of the key elements of keeping the project on track is determining *what* should actually be measured to determine the status of the project. Too often, a demand for concrete data about project performance comes only after a project is struggling, and at that point, speed takes precedence over spending an appropriate amount of time determining the most effective data to measure.

Green/yellow/red charts are a nice way to quickly ascertain statuses in a user-friendly form, but only when everyone reading the chart is aware of the exact metric being measured, and exactly what each color means. A very different course of action may be required if a "red" status indicates something is 50 percent complete versus 4 percent complete.

Metrics should be determined as early as possible in the project lifecycle, preferably in the blueprint phase, before plans are developed and before the full project team comes on board. Since project plans, team structures, and work schedules will all be derived from these metrics, ensuring they are well thought out and appropriately "set in stone" before the team expands and begins to march toward project completion will ensure every team member knows where the project stands at all times.

So, what should actually be measured to ensure a project is on track for delivering its expected organizational value? One of the easiest routes is to work backward and start with the question, "What does success look like?" Aside from a large go-live party with free-flowing beverages and finger food, asking this question should drive you toward key pieces of functionality or organizational objectives that must be in place for the project to be considered a success. For example, if you are delivering a new logistics system, one of the measures of success might be that orders will leave the warehouse 30 percent faster than by using the old system. This measure of success, flushed out in further detail, might reveal that one of the key bottlenecks in current systems is the time it takes for the order to be sent from the call center to the warehouse. Therefore, one of your metrics might be ensuring complete orders are transmitted from the call center to the warehouse in under 10 minutes.

This measure would then lead to instituting some kind of benchmarking process that can be run as the new systems and processes are deployed, to track the current progress of the project toward that one measure of success. Contrast this process to the usual standard in large IT projects of tracking progress through deliverables. Large projects often consider documentation and administrative tasks deliverables, and then measure success on what percentage of those deliverables have been completed.

Tracking a project based on deliverables in this sense is exceedingly dangerous. One hundred percent of deliverables can be completed, but this may not indicate the project has successfully completed its organizational objective—in our example, to ship packages 30 percent faster. Compare the "Deliverable" model to the "Project Success" model in Exhibit 6.2 for examples of a traditional deliverable-based metric and the corresponding metric generated by asking, "What does success look like?"

Notice that the deliverable model metrics all focus on the completion of a specific task that is not directly tied to a required organizational objective. While completing the training documentation

EXHIBIT 6.2

Deliverable vs. Project Success Model Metrics

Deliverable Model Metric	Project Success Model Metric
100% of test cases executed	Orders shipped at least 30% faster in test system
100% of functional specifications completed	10% of effort required to run a benchmark on shipping orders in the new system
Training documentation completed	Sample group of users and project team report training documentation is 90% satisfactory or greater
Post-implementation support plan completed	Post-implementation support team trained, support processes in place, and dry-run completed

certainly moves the project toward success, no component of that measurement ensures the training documentation meets organizational objectives. Rather than asking if we have a completed house to live in, the deliverables model is asking if the carpenter has a complete set of chisels.

In the same vein, completing plans or various pieces of project documentation moves the project forward in a general sense, but is not tied to any concrete organizational objective. Complete functional specifications may or may not contain the appropriate level of detail to allow for a thorough initial benchmarking of the shipment process. Reporting that all the documentation is complete gives a false sense of project status. What does "complete" mean in this sense and how does it benefit the organization?

Determining a robust set of objectives to fit within the Project Success models is easier than it sounds. Nearly every large undertaking has a project charter, or cost/benefit analysis that details expected organizational savings. While some may be high level—for example, "Reduce IT spending by 5 percent"—the exercise of breaking down each high-level benefit into measurable components provides two valuable pieces of information. First, this exercise validates the assumptions that are driving the investment in the project. If an assertion that IT spending will be reduced by 5 percent is made, but no measurable data points exist to support that assertion, you may become a corporate hero by killing a potential runaway project before it even starts. Second, drilling each high-level organizational objective into measurable metrics brings a results-based culture to your project team from its inception to project close. No longer are team members striving toward satisfying a methodology, but they can see directly how their efforts are driving toward corporate objectives. Every project has "cheerleading" sessions expounding on the wonderful work of the team and how it will benefit the company in the long term, but how many projects have you presided over in which each team member knows how much of the bottom line his or her efforts are contributing to?

Exhibit 6.3 shows a sample breakdown of a Project Charter-level organizational objective into its constituent components. Note that each is assigned a value or a contribution percentage to the overall ROI, both IT-related components and non–IT-related components of the complete project. This exercise provides solid financial data as inputs into the management process, and validates the assumptions that were made in calculating ROI. This process also further cements the transition of IT from technologists to purveyors of organizational

EXHIBIT 6.3

Metric Development Process

```
                    ┌──────────────┐
                    │   Reduce     │
                    │  Operating   │
                    │ Expenses by  │
                    │    $2.5M     │
                    └──────┬───────┘
              ┌────────────┴────────────┐
              │                         │
      ┌───────┴──────┐          ┌───────┴──────────┐
      │Cut Logistics │          │Reduce Personnel  │    ┌──────────────────┐
      │Costs by $1M  │          │Costs by $0.5M    │    │  Increase Call    │
      └───────┬──────┘          └───────┬──────────┘    │Center Profitability│
              │                         │               │    by $1M         │
   ┌──────────┤              ┌──────────┤               └──────────────────┘
   │          │              │          │
┌──┴───┐ ┌────┴───┐ ┌────┐ ┌─┴────┐ ┌───┴──────┐
│New   │ │Reduce  │ │Close│ │New HR│ │Outsource │
│Shipping│Cycle   │ │Ware-│ │System│ │Payroll   │
│System│ │Time 25%│ │house│ │(80%  │ │(20%      │
│(30%  │ │(40%    │ │(30% │ │contri│ │contribu- │
│contri│ │contri- │ │contr│ │bution│ │tion      │
│bution│ │bution  │ │ibu- │ │margin│ │margin)   │
│margin)│margin) │ │tion │ │)     │ │          │
└──────┘ └────────┘ │margi│ └──────┘ └──────────┘
                    │n)   │
                    └─────┘
```

value and builds consensus for the project, as far more involvement from the financial and operational arms of the organization is required to accurately flush out the project's ROI.

You can use any number of brainstorming tools to help "decompose" the project's value into constituent pieces. How do you know when you have reached the right level of detail? Follow the "MAD" rule.

A metric must be MAD:

Measurable: Looks for items that can be tracked to indicate success of the metric, measurable, for example, in minutes, items shipped, dollars, or units produced. Avoid the "traffic-light syndrome" of using gut feelings to drive a project.

Actionable: You can clearly define a list of tasks that must be completed to accomplish the objective.

Dollar-oriented: This separates a metric from a task or deliverable. Reducing helpdesk costs by 5 percent is a metric with a hard cost savings. Completing training on how to use the new trouble ticket system has no immediate measurable monetary impact to the business, but might be an appropriate task associated with reducing helpdesk costs. While completing a particular deliverable is measurable and actionable, it is not directly tied to organizational savings, and therefore is not an appropriate metric.

Managing to the Metrics

Once you have decomposed ROI into a more granular level, eventually you will have a collection of measurable objectives that tie back to the overall organizational goal of a project. Instead of tracking documentation, one of the metrics might be the time between when an order is taken by customer service, and when it is validated and printed in the warehouse. Furthermore, as you decompose ROI and map a contribution margin to each metric, a hard dollar value becomes associated with each item that then rolls up to overall organizational value.

Pause for a moment and consider the previous paragraph, as it marks a dramatic shift for most IT organizations. By mapping ROI directly to its constituent, measurable parts, IT is no longer an organizational cost center, but a department that creates true, *measurable* value for the organization. Discussions about IT projects are rooted in quantifiable value rather than fuzzy numbers and difficult justifications for expenditures. IT has become a value engine.

This focus on value must then be driven down to all levels of the IT organization. Metrics become the objectives passed down to lower-level managers, project managers allocate tasks and manage against the metrics, and projects are tracked based on their current level of realized ROI. Again, deliverables are used as a tool to complete metrics, rather than an objective in and of themselves. This shift in management, while seemingly a subtle distinction, completely shifts the way an IT project is tracked. Each task now rolls up to a metric that has a defined organizational value. Rather than trying to "meet the dates," and then waiting and hoping to see if a project delivers its expected value, a snapshot of project status at any given time will show immediately how much organizational value will be derived by the project's current state.

Traditional project planning generally tied tasks to a specific deliverable, milestone, or project phase. Using traditional planning tools, tasks were assigned a level of effort, and rolled up to higher-level tasks, eventually providing an overall level of effort required to complete the project, and an associated current percentage completion. While certainly better than the tendency for IT projects to measure status without any hard data, these plans consistently measured the wrong thing: task completion versus value delivery.

Examine the simple project plan in Exhibit 6.4. Each task has a work effort assigned in days, dependencies assigned, and a current level of completion. Based on the relationship between tasks, one would conclude the project is 71 percent complete. This might be considered great news if only 50 percent of the budget and time allocated to these tasks had been consumed. However, looking at this plan through the lens of organizational value does not indicate what, if anything, the project has realized in terms of the measurable organizational benefit.

EXHIBIT 6.4

Traditional Demo Plan

ID	❶	Task Name	Duration	Predecessors	% Complete
1		**System Build**	**72 days**		**71%**
2	✔	Engage stakeholders	2 days		100%
3	✔	Complete functional specifications	40 days		100%
4	✔	Deliver specifications to developers	2 days	3	100%
5		Approve functional specs	5 days	4	75%
6	✔	Prepare development environment	15 days		100%
7		Complete development	25 days	6,5	0%

EXHIBIT 6.5

Value Demo Plan

ID	●	Task Name	Duration	Prede-cessors	Est. Org. Value	Realized Value	% Complete
1		**System Build**	**72 days**		**$10,000.00**	**$0.00**	**71%**
2	✔	Engage stakeholders	2 days		$0.00	$0.00	100%
3	✔	Complete functional specifications	40 days		$0.00	$0.00	100%
4	✔	Deliver specifications to developers	2 days	3	$0.00	$0.00	100%
5		Approve functional specs	5 days	4	$0.00	$0.00	75%
6	✔	Prepare development environment	15 days		$0.00	$0.00	100%
7		Complete development	25 days	6,5	$10,000.00	$0.00	0%

Contrast the plan in Exhibit 6.4 with that in Exhibit 6.5. If the aim of this project is to deliver a system that can be used to test new functionality that delivers measurable value to the organization, no value will be realized until the test system is complete. While the tasks in the second plan and work effort to complete the project remain the same, notice that no organizational value has been realized.

An obvious question based on the plan in Exhibit 6.5 would be, "Don't all projects and 'project success' metrics realize their value only when all tasks are complete?" The answer, of course, is yes, since each element of the ROI decomposition ends up being a metric, and unless you have broken ROI down into too granular a level, each metric will require several tasks to accomplish the objective measured by the metric.

Initially, this may appear to be a self-defeating method of tracking projects. If no organizational value is realized until nearly all tasks behind a metric are complete, how will the team ever get a sense of accomplishment? This shift of focus from task "completeness" to value delivery is exactly what makes this method of tracking a project so powerful. While you will no longer have artificial milestones as celebration points, focus will shift to the end game, with its associated organizational value, versus focusing on project-related deadlines that may not accomplish anything for the company as a whole.

This method also focuses project managers and their subordinates on pursuing objectives based on their value, rather than on some vendor methodology or arbitrary phased approach. If the tasks associated with a low-value metric are slipping, managers can easily make a decision to cannibalize resources for a higher-value task, or allocate the slipping task to a later phase. Again, decisions are made from a perspective of value to the company, rather than completing a deliverable or delivering functionality that appeals to individual prerogative.

Beyond the Numbers: The "Gut Check"

Much of the strategy around delivering strategic projects in the Breakthrough IT organization centers on quantifying the value of major project components, and ensuring each component delivers against that proposed value. While this exercise ensures a detailed understanding of the components that make up a project's value, it is a robust analytical process that can be time consuming. While the Breakthrough IT organization strives to quantify the value it delivers, this is not to suggest that the combined experience of the IT organization should be ignored. Subjecting whole projects, or elements of a strategic project, to an organizational "gut check" may allow components of the project to be dismissed before conducting any detailed analysis of the returns of that project.

A gut check may also reveal previously unstated assumptions behind an ROI calculation that may represent a critical dependency or failure point of a project, which can then be broken out and tracked. In an organization with a proven track record of delivering projects, the gut check may suffice in all but the most complex projects, and detailed ROI analysis may be bypassed in the interest of time. This assumption relies on IT's past experience, and should not be disconnected from analyzing past projects to see if returns match the original expectations. If the organization does not check its past performance, there is little in terms of hard numbers to quantify the success of IT, or ensure accurate ROI predictions in the future.

Delivering the Goods

As you transition existing and new projects to a decomposed ROI method of tracking and management, you reach the holy grail of project portfolio management. Each individual project is broken down into constituent parts, each with a specific, measurable metric with a hard figure attached representing value to the business. At budgeting time, projects are no longer just an expense item, but now have a corresponding value attached, complete with a current "state of the union" indicating the amount of value that has already been realized, and the remaining value yet to be delivered.

The chart of "fuzzy numbers" and red/yellow/green "feeling-based" metrics pictured in the beginning of the chapter can be replaced by something similar to Exhibit 6.6.

Rather than busy text and colored boxes attempting to obfuscate any hint of what is actually happening with a particular project, the

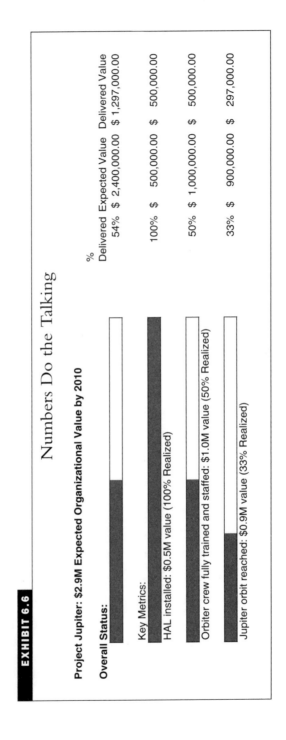

EXHIBIT 6.6

Numbers Do the Talking

Project Jupiter: $2.9M Expected Organizational Value by 2010

	% Delivered	Expected Value	Delivered Value
Overall Status:	54%	$ 2,400,000.00	$ 1,297,000.00
Key Metrics:			
HAL installed: $0.5M value (100% Realized)	100%	$ 500,000.00	$ 500,000.00
Orbiter crew fully trained and staffed: $1.0M value (50% Realized)	50%	$ 1,000,000.00	$ 500,000.00
Jupiter orbit reached: $0.9M value (33% Realized)	33%	$ 900,000.00	$ 297,000.00

simple chart in Exhibit 6.6 can provide an overview of each project in your portfolio, with the status of each. Obscure deliverables and technology terms are distilled into organizational value; they become a tool everyone in the executive suite can quickly grasp and use to make decisions. A column with spend data for each project and its associated components can further sharpen the focus of this chart, providing real ROI data for each element of a project. Increased spending on a particular project can be easily justified, or a decision to scrap an underperforming project can be made more quickly, based primarily on fact rather than hearsay.

This approach puts IT projects in a similar light to other strategic projects occurring in the organization. Ongoing IT operations designed to maintain and expand existing infrastructure can be reported as more traditional expense items, heightening the separation of strategic versus maintenance expenses.

Part of the transition of IT from a commodity to a strategic engine involves educating other executives, and proving that the IT organization can actually deliver on the ROI it has forecast and assigned to various projects. By maintaining a rigid focus on business drivers for technology, rather than the actual technology, IT becomes more accessible and justifiable to the organization as a whole. It should be irrelevant in the C-suite whether XML, SOAP, or Linux is powering the logistics infrastructure, yet everyone will sit up straight in his or her chair when it is revealed that a strategic IT effort reduced supply chain expenses by 6 percent over two years.

Developing projects married to organizational value, and managing to the resulting metrics lays the groundwork for success. Reporting based on those metrics with a focus on organizational value puts IT into a strategic context, beginning the process of proving that IT is an engine for organizational value rather than yet another ongoing expense. Developing a track record of success and learning from failure are the final pieces of the puzzle. Partnerships between IT and the rest of the corporation will further cement this transition. As projects move toward maturity, IT and finance should constantly be evaluating the returns on investment and analyzing any variances. Were original estimates too conservative or pessimistic? Did the project fail in some area that resulted in less value to the organization? Exhibit 6.7 provides a simplified decision tree for studying variances in expected and actual ROI.

As the corporation matures and develops competencies in accurately estimating ROI and determining metrics tied to decomposed ROI, combined with solid project execution, IT will be seen as an investment with generally reliable returns. No longer is executive leadership relegated to reviewing color charts and hearing fuzzy predictions about the results of IT spending.

 ACTION POINTS

Action points provide concrete steps you can use to begin implementing ideas from this chapter. For this chapter, the action points are:

- Pick one or two projects that are in the proposal stages or only recently begun as a testing ground for managing via "decomposed ROI." Clearly explain the strategy for this management style to project managers and ensure they relay this information to their team.

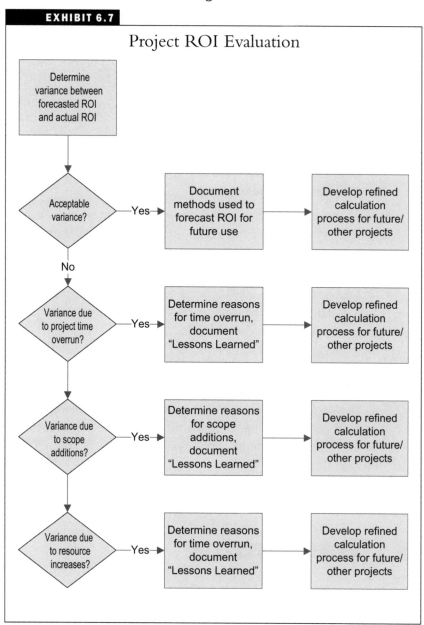

EXHIBIT 6.7

Project ROI Evaluation

- Take the overall ROI for your test projects, and partner IT and corporate finance to decompose overall ROI into metrics that meet the MAD criteria (Measurable, Actionable, and Dollar-based).

- Feed the MAD metrics to your project manager(s) for use in developing their detailed planning, and begin using these metrics for status reporting.

- Begin reporting IT project status based on organizational value for the sample group of projects. Capture feedback as to the value of the new management and reporting style and determine if it is effective for your organization.

- As the company gains confidence in project reporting based on organizational value, consider transitioning other ongoing projects to this method. At this point, newer, nimbler projects are preferable to very large projects or those near the end of their implementation lifecycle.

- In executive meetings, facilitate discussions on new business strategies or areas in which IT can generate organizational value. Begin suggesting the application of strategic IT, based on the ROI delivered by enabling a particular business process through IT.

EXECUTIVE SUMMARY

Moving IT from a corporate expense to a strategic expenditure, and transitioning the role of IT from technologists to strategic visionaries requires changing the way you and your fellow executives think about IT projects. Managing and reporting on projects based on deliver-

EXECUTIVE SUMMARY (CONTINUED)

ables or qualitative measures does not engender confidence in IT as a purveyor of strategy. Projects must be tied to strategic business objectives, each objective having a corresponding monetary figure that represents the value to the organization that will be realized upon completion of the objective. "Decomposing" the ROI of the overall project and marrying each component to a metric allows projects to be managed and their status viewed in terms of organizational value, not an arbitrary milestone that contributes nothing to the company's bottom line.

As projects are moved from deliverable-based milestones to "Project Success"–based metrics, tasks are allocated based on realizing organizational value. A subtle shift in project management occurs, as all tasks feed into delivering measurable, actionable, and dollar-based results. No longer is the project team focused on project tasks that exist in a vacuum, but they can directly see how tasks deliver value to the organization. Changes in the project's schedule or scope now tie back to value-based metrics, providing management with feedback on the status of the project in terms of business objectives and business value.

As your IT department builds its competencies in these areas, it can improve on its ability to predict and manage to metrics based on decomposed ROI. Upon completing a project, analysis can be done to determine the accuracy of the metrics and how well they were met by the project. As competency improves, returns on strategic IT investment can be more accurately predicted, making IT investment a more reliable bet than other areas of strategic spending. As this process becomes increasingly refined, IT will be seen as a reliable point of delivery for organizational strategy, and the organization's ability to implement and drive strategy through technology will become increasingly apparent.

CHAPTER 7

Pushing Water Uphill

Driving Organizational Change from the C-Suite

The Greek philosophers knew a thing or two about the modern corporation, with Heraclitus penning the famous line, "Nothing endures but change." With all the talk about organizational change, change management, and process change, the concern and emphasis on change seems both obvious and overdone, yet business history provides plenty of examples at the macro level of different reactions to change.

Companies such as Polaroid created a technology that defined an industry, developing and successfully selling instant cameras that could produce photographs moments after the shutter was clicked. With dominant market share, and a well-protected proprietary technology, they were a staple from fashion photographers to the aisles of mom-and-pop corner stores. Polaroid was a successfully run company, yet it did not react to external changes in the market with the advent of digital photography. This failure to react to change caused Polaroid to abandon its shiny headquarters building on the Charles River near Boston to become little more than a holding company for various patents and trademarks.

At the opposite end of the spectrum are companies that did not just react to changes in the market, but initiated the change, forcing competitors to adapt on their terms. Companies like Apple and Google introduced products and services that were not new, but redefined portable music and Internet searching. Competitors now look to the Apples and Googles of the world for their inspiration, and wonder what process or product these dynamos will produce next, forcing a reaction across the competitive landscape.

At the individual company level, change is easier to institute and control since we are dealing with a smaller population and can control many of the factors that lead to acceptance or rejection of an organizational change, be it a new strategy, process, project, or combination thereof. Precipitating change is almost too easy. With a few e-mails or boardroom conversations, corporate policies can change overnight. External factors, be they violent global conflict or a competitor introducing an industry-changing product, also can foist change upon a corporation in a matter of minutes. How the company reacts to these changes, and ensures that the organization quickly migrates to this new business environment with the least amount of organizational "pain" is the essence of this chapter.

What Is "Change Management?"

Like many buzzwords, the term "change management" has picked up so much baggage and is so frequently used and misused that it ceases to have an understandable meaning. The change we are concerned about in the context of the Breakthrough IT organization is that which is initiated by the C-suite. This could be the change associated with a strategic project, or a new strategy that has been initiated due to events in the external environment. The Breakthrough IT organization, which derives its value primarily through executing strategic projects, is in a unique position to handle change. Projects are inherently different from business as usual, and even without the formal moniker of "change management," the Breakthrough IT shop likely has a great deal of experience in this area.

Simply put, change management comprises several broad areas:

- Understanding a particular change, and determining who will be affected and what the impact to each party will be

- Explaining the change to each affected party, and appealing to their self-interest to encourage the party to adapt to the new environment

- Helping the affected parties transition from the old way of doing things to the new "business as usual"

As depicted in the simple flowchart in Exhibit 7.1, this is often a cyclical process and not a one-time activity or box that can be checked off on a project plan. Simply put, change management is the constant process of helping your people adapt to change.

Change management is often confused with some of its component activities, like training or communications, and is passed to junior

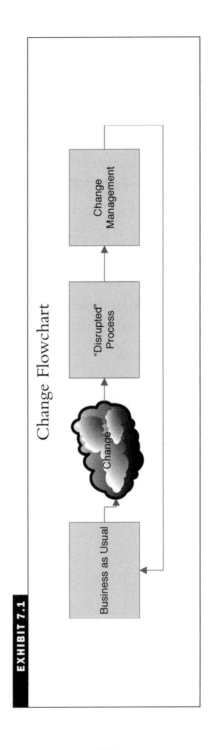

EXHIBIT 7.1

Change Flowchart

personnel or a specific team. While training is the key to helping affected employees adapt to organizational change, by itself it is not change management. True change management is not one particular team or business unit; rather, it is the responsibility of many people within the organization, starting at the very top, in the C-suite.

While there are occasional grassroots changes in corporate strategy that meet with internal success and widespread acclaim, support for change should generally begin at the top of an organization. While grassroots change management efforts are critical to the overall success of a project, attempting to institute change without support at the highest levels of the organization can be extremely difficult. One particularly critical area is the loss of productivity associated with a change in the way a company does business. This is one of the many prices of changing a process, especially if the process being changed has become entrenched in the organization and the new processes are significantly different from the old. Without support at the highest levels in the organization, an otherwise well-intentioned project could be abandoned just when it is on the cusp of success as productivity drops without a corresponding expectation and understanding of the drop by senior management.

The Role of the CIO in Change Management

In the Breakthrough IT organization, IT and the CIO are in a unique position to drive change. As IT develops its acumen in executing business strategy developed in the C-suite, and implements and optimizes processes at a business unit level, it finds itself serving as a bridge between the highest level of the organization and those directly affected by changes to the way the company does business. As mentioned in previous chapters, as the CIO becomes a trusted peer to colleagues in the C-suite, he or she has increasing access and input on strategic decisions. The CIO can also use his or her experience in implementing strategic projects to gauge the reactions of line-level employees and managers to proposed change, providing exceptionally valuable input into these strategic discussions.

With projects evaluated as part of a larger project portfolio focused on their individual ROI, and ongoing operations appropriately sourced, change management becomes one of the primary responsibilities of the Breakthrough CIO. The CIO has access to the high-level strategic and operational objectives of the corporation, and uses this information to identify and execute projects, and to ensure the organization as a whole accepts and adapts to these new ways of doing business. In short, for any organizational change that is executed and managed by the Breakthrough IT organization, the CIO becomes the primary person responsible for change management.

In combination with process reengineering expertise, the CIO should field a cadre of change experts on each project team. This group need not be a special, standalone team; rather, those directly responsible for implementing new processes and technologies should also be able to analyze the effect these changes will have on the recipients of the new process. Whether these impacts can be mitigated through extensive training, an internal "marketing" program, or through more hard-line measures, those on the front lines of process change are best equipped to identify these requirements and hand them off to the appropriate dedicated resources, such as trainers. The CIO's responsibility in this process is communicating the high-level objectives associated with each change to those on the front lines, and monitoring the overall state of the business—how well it is adapting to the new way of conducting "business as usual."

The Role of the CEO in Change Management

While the CIO is given primary responsibility for overseeing change management, the CEO has a more interesting dynamic. The CEO effectively wears two hats, being the ultimate initiator of change, and the "celebrity spokesperson" within the organization, serving as an advocate for everything from sweeping changes in the company to the latest strategic project being driven by the Breakthrough IT shop.

The first role is self-explanatory. With obligations to the Board, customers, shareholders, and employees, the CEO must take their concerns, external market factors, and his or her own instincts, and determine how to make the corporation more successful. For sweeping changes in the company's strategy, CEOs develop a strategic plan, pitch that plan to all concerned parties, and build the case for its acceptance. Finally, they initiate the appropriate activities to execute on that plan. For more rudimentary decisions, the CEO may unilaterally initiate change, or bring about change by bestowing the final approval to a project as part of the project selection committee. When executing strategic projects, the CEO generally institutes the change process, while the CIO provides the operational oversight to ensure the change is successfully executed.

This role is straightforward, as CEOs have been tasked as the ultimate decision makers since the dawn of the modern corporation. What is new in the Breakthrough IT organization is the relationship between the CEO and CIO, one as initiator and one as the manager of change. If your organization is well on its way to Breakthrough status, the CIO has already established him- or herself as a business-savvy resource, and this role becomes a natural extension. If this trust is lacking, and the CIO is not yet able to sit at the table with senior management, there will be a disconnect between the CEO as the institutor of change and IT's process experts who are on the front lines of delivering the new way of doing business and managing the transition.

The second, often overlooked role of the CEO is that of celebrity spokesperson for any large-scale change effort. Celebrity spokespeople have been used for everything from pitching products to telling children to avoid smoking, and in the corporate environment, the most accessible celebrity is the CEO. The CEO is in a unique position as the ultimate day-to-day leader of the company, and frequently has contact with customers, shareholders, and the Board and can frame change from multiple perspectives. Using the CEO as a spokesperson can convey several important messages:

- This change is important and being watched from the highest levels of the organization: the CEO, Board, shareholders, and customers.

- Those parties implementing and experiencing the change have the support of the aforementioned groups.

- This change is the right thing to do in a larger organizational context, and augments the overall strategy of the corporation.

- The CEO acknowledges that change is difficult, and that there will be bumps in the road before it is fully implemented and becomes business as usual.

The mere appearance of the CEO at most companies makes a bold statement about the importance of a particular effort, and the support behind that effort. Other corporate leaders may also have a similar impact, although it is rarely as strong as a message directly from the CEO and often does not convey the broader significance of a project to those involved.

Change Management at the Line Level

Much of this chapter has focused on the importance of initiating and driving change from the highest levels of an organization. While this is both necessary and advantageous, any organizational changes must be understood and carefully implemented with the people who will be directly affected by the change in the organization. Line-level employees and managers are generally the ones who will have to change their daily routine the most to accommodate new systems, processes, or policies, and therefore, their support is critical to implementing any change.

Three Cheers for Change

The most effective tool for instituting change at this level is a group of "evangelist" users; people who are respected by their peers and truly believe in the positive impact the change will engender. Think of this as your "cheerleading squad," who will augment the positive messages coming from the top of the organization with pragmatic support, ensuring that your efforts to change the company are not perceived as the latest management fad being rammed down the throats of the peons by their superiors in the corner office.

Identifying this group is straightforward, and they should be handpicked down the chain of command. The CIO and business unit leaders should select a group of trusted managers, who then select two or three line-level employees to serve as cheerleaders. Often called "super users," "power users," or some other term, their primary role in the early phases of any change management effort is simply to gain an understanding of the benefits, drawbacks, and changes to their daily routine that will be required, and share this information with their colleagues. It is preferable to select these cheerleaders based on past performance rather than asking for volunteers, or allowing management to select them from a pool of willing volunteers. Criteria to look for in "change cheerleaders" are:

- Respected by their colleagues. This lends credence to their message and stifles the sense that something is being done *to* them rather than *for* them.

- Know the current business process, but see the value in the future state.

- A person who has gone through a change effort in the past rather than someone who has performed the same job for decades.

- Someone who is upbeat and positive, while remaining honest, who will reflect the change effort in a positive light without sugarcoating any potential pain during the implementation of the new process.

For a radically new process, perhaps the most important criteria are finding a "true believer" in the change that is being instituted, and someone who is respected by his or her colleagues. The more radical the change, the more evangelists you need at all levels of the organization. These change cheerleaders need not filter everything through a positive lens, however. Change is usually difficult, and a degree of struggle is required to achieve most meaningful changes. Acknowledging this pain, and more importantly conveying the message that the pain is expected, and any resultant decreases in productivity planned for, augments the enthusiasm for the future state with pragmatic acknowledgment of the effort that will be required to get there.

Influencing Change 101

There are countless books and theories about how to encourage people to change. From the latest diet fad to massive process reengineering efforts, theories abound. While there are good ideas nestled in the many tomes on change, the crux of influencing people to change is appealing to the self-interest of those impacted by the change. Individuals, on their own or working together in a large organization, generally do not like to change. It disrupts their lives, often requires abandoning deeply engrained habits, and necessitates learning an entirely new way of doing things. Change generates inefficiency and creates fear, as everything you once understood and had influence over is reordered and upset. Countering this fear requires convincing those affected that the new state of the world will be more appealing than the old, at an individual level.

Organizations often make compelling arguments about the benefits of change to the collective organization. At its worst, change management consists of sending banal, corporate council–approved memos announcing a layoff in one breath, and then expounding for several sentences about how the layoff really is the best thing for the company, its shareholders, and the employees who just lost their livelihood. Whether that is the case or not, a faceless memo expounding on the collective good does little to appease the manager who watches a trusted supervisor pack up his or her desk, or the factory workers who see their buddy next to them on the line dismissed after working together for 20 years. In the same manner, organizational change efforts that highlight the collective good, when individuals see only the associated pain and fear, are likely to garner little support. On the other hand, change efforts that appeal to each employee on an individual level and demonstrate how their career and working life will be improved by the change are vastly more likely to succeed.

Appealing to individuals' self-interest can generally be accomplished through one of two means, or a combination of the two. First, the company can positively reward those who adapt to the "new world" the most effectively, either through compensation, advancement, recognition, or some combination thereof. This positive reinforcement generally encourages those who are more willing to change, and if you can effectively demonstrate the appeal of the change to each impacted person's self-interest, you can be very effective at using positive reinforcement.

Where positive reinforcement fails is that the fear of change can often outweigh any benefits that accompany its adoption. If an employee of the company is a high performer, or feels safe in his or her position, that person has little incentive to change, and the appeal to his or her self-interest must be all the more dramatic. In many cases, entrenched managers, people at the end of their careers, or high-performing sales executives are the most difficult groups in which to implement organizational change. These groups are often rewarded based on very narrow criteria, or have protected status and have been shielded from past change efforts. To appeal to groups like these, you must make the appeal to their self-interest so compelling that it cannot be refused, or make the old way of doing things so unappealing as to force them to change by using negative reinforcement.

Negative reinforcement is often frowned upon as a tool to institute change, as it is seen as beating people into submission. While no one wants to work under the reign of a tyrannical dictatorship, at the end of the day if the only way to appeal to an individual's self-interest is to threaten his or her compensation, status, or advancement potential, and the change that is being instituted is overwhelmingly valuable to the organization as a whole, negative reinforcement is a powerful tool that should not be abandoned simply for its perception as a tool of tyrants.

Organizational change rarely benefits every soul within the corporation, and there will always be some group within the company that must take on additional work with little additional glory for the benefit of the company as a whole. While flowery presentations of the myriad benefits will win the hearts and minds of a few individuals in these types of positions, the majority will likely resist the change. It is these types of groups where negative reinforcement can be most effective, especially when combined with positive reinforcement. Essentially, you are punishing the old behavior, while rewarding the new behavior. Regardless of the benefits or lack thereof to the new way of doing business at the individual level, the organization must make the old way of working as unappealing as possible, forcing change by appealing primarily to the self-interest of the affected employees.

A mistake frequently made in a process or technology change project is not making corresponding changes in the reward and punishment systems that drive employees' compensation and advancement possibilities. Old models have frequently been tuned over the years to encourage employees to work within the boundaries of the old processes and technologies, and logic would dictate that leaving these old structures in place while encouraging a new behavior is likely a recipe for disaster.

Tuning the Instrument: Levers to Institute Change

The tomes on managing change often suggest that it can be encouraged through various levers: external influences that can modify behavior. Compensation is the classic lever, assuming that providing monetary reward for the behaviors you wish to encourage will cause employees to exhibit those behaviors. While compensation is an obvious lever, it is not as effective as one might think. Compensation is the working world's equivalent of water, food, and shelter, essential to life and sorely missed when it is gone, but generally not a concern as long as it is present in adequate levels.

Bonuses, advancement opportunities, and other outward signs of status and success within the corporation are generally more highly prized by competitive employees. As the levers that publicly recognize employees for meeting the new definitions of high performance are likely to be more highly prized, they are thus more effective in bringing about change.

A detailed plan on how to manipulate the right levers to institute change is beyond the scope of this book; however, the basic premise is that levers should accomplish the following:

- Make it rewarding to adopt the new process.
- Publicly celebrate those who adapt to the new way of working, through advancement opportunities, bonuses, commissions, etc.
- Make the old way of working as unappealing as possible.
- Build an organizational "wall" around the old processes and methodologies that makes change the path of least resistance. Countless studies show that people generally prefer the routine to uncertainty, and if your change management process makes the routine too easy to continue, there is little incentive to adapt to the new way of doing business.

While much of the talk of change management focuses on human nature, and gentle encouragement of employees toward the new way of working, there must be a willingness to use extreme tactics should the need arise. If a project is truly critical to a company's success, and an integral part of the project portfolio, there should be a process in place to identify those who do not adapt to the new way of working, and provide stern discipline and coaching, followed by an internal transfer or firing. If a single person is allowed to avoid change, through sheer stubbornness or political pressure, all the public relations and communications efforts made by the CEO on down will be rendered moot. This unpleasant aspect of change management should not be overlooked, especially when implementing projects that involve traditionally difficult groups like marketing and sales. If the company does not have the collective stomach to force change when gentler means do not suffice, a rebellion in the ranks can destroy years of effort and waste millions of dollars.

The End of Business as Usual

By its very nature, change is disruptive. From the simplest IT project to upgrade a desktop application, to a massive process reengineering and systems implementation project, the new processes and technical tools will disrupt the day-to-day lives and productivity of those who must use them. Effective change also requires a cadre of experts to monitor and support the process, and the attention of executives in the C-suite, robbing their focus on other matters for a time to ensure the success of the venture. This dip in productivity can be small and fairly quick, or it can be massive, taking several weeks or months until productivity returns to the levels it was at before any new processes or tools were implemented. Learning any modified skill is similar, from a refined golf swing to a perfectly pronounced French sonnet. One must first "unlearn" his or her previous technique, and then spend a period of time adopting the new technique, trading short-term lack of competency for longer-term superior performance.

Neglecting to plan for this productivity dip and period of corporate loss of focus is one of the central risks in managing change. If this dip is accounted for, and implementations planned to minimize the adverse effects from turning the eyes of the company inward, success is far more likely than with picking an arbitrary date and hoping for the best. To minimize the effect of this learning period:

- Spend a significant amount of time, money, and painstaking effort during the testing and training portions of any project. You can rarely overtest a new system or process, nor can you overtrain those who will be using them.

- Have actual users involved in all stages of the project, from its initial conception through testing. Organizational surprises translate to significant dips in productivity and slower user acceptance. Involving users will help unearth any of these potential surprises at an earlier stage of the project, providing time to develop a solution.

- Plan implementation dates for historically slow times of the year to avoid taking an internal focus while significant market or economic changes occur.

- Create detailed contingency plans for various levels of productivity loss, and plan accordingly. Contract for temporary help, or develop processes that can offload lower-priority work while the new way of working takes root.

- Spread the word at every level of the organization and across business units that a strategic project will affect service levels, stress levels, and all aspects of "business as usual" well in advance of the implementation of the new processes or tools. Encourage related business units to create contingency plans should the productivity of a supporting business unit fall significantly.

Managing change often blurs the line between an art and a science. Significant planning and logistical support are required, along with several contingency plans and monitoring tools. These tools must be combined with a healthy understanding of human nature, organizational politics, and external market forces. Clearly, the tasks required to successfully implement change cover a broad range of skills, and extend well beyond the traditional boundaries of training and communications. Every person involved with a strategic project plays some role in the change management process, from analysts who can gauge the acceptance of a new process at the line level and serve as the "ears on the street," to the CEO who serves as a mouthpiece for the project across the company.

Change management also serves as a checkpoint for a project, and can indicate that changing internal or external circumstances have made a project no longer relevant in its current guise. Change efforts can uncover facts that may have been previously glossed over or unclear, and can provide an early warning sign of an unsuccessful project that may not be reflected in ROI numbers or project management reports until a later date.

Successfully instituting change requires an appeal to each employee's self-interest. For many employees, this will involve providing superior rewards for new behaviors versus the old, thus encouraging adoption of new processes and tools. For some, change management will require difficult discussions and perhaps dismissing an otherwise successful employee who simply refuses to adapt to the new way of working.

Unwavering support from the highest levels of the organization must be tempered with rational explanations of the new way of conducting business at the lowest levels of the organization, both building support and recognizing that the change process will be painful and disruptive to the organization immediately after being rolled out. The Breakthrough IT organization is a central driver of change. It cannot be successful simply by managing a project portfolio and delivering new processes and tools; rather, it must be both empowered and capable of changing the way each employee in the company works.

ACTION POINTS

Action points provide concrete steps you can use to begin implementing ideas from this chapter. For this chapter, the action points are:

- Initiate discussions among the C-level executives and discuss the role of each in instituting organizational change. Is the CIO capable of driving change? Has the CEO been an effective champion of previous change efforts?

- Perform an analysis of several past projects, including at least one pure process change project, one pure technology project, and one project that included components of each. How well did each manage organizational change? Capture any lessons learned and look to where they can be applied to current projects.

- Identify any "change agents": employees who have served as evangelists for past change efforts, spreading positive news about upcoming efforts while providing pragmatic advice about how the daily lives of employees will be affected. Consider using these people on future projects or asking for their help in identifying other change agents.

- Look at any formal change management organizations within the PMO or current projects. Is change management merely serving as a fancy title for a training group, or are these people truly helping to facilitate organizational change?

- Investigate previous productivity dips due to large process and systems projects. How were they planned for and mitigated?

ACTION POINTS (CONTINUED)

- Ensure the PMO has a formal process for estimating productivity loss and helping the affected business units to develop contingency plans, such as hiring temporary employees or decreasing service-level agreements.

- Analyze past training and testing efforts. Were users involved heavily with each? Were realistic business scenarios modeled and tested? Were users satisfied with the training they received and was it effective, or should the mix between formal training and on-the-job learning be modified?

 EXECUTIVE SUMMARY

Change management is the science (and art) of effectively implementing that pesky and omnipresent specter: change. Effective change management is the key to the Breakthrough IT organization. Since Breakthrough IT is tied to the successful implementation of strategic projects, facilitating the efficient adoption of the new processes and tools they deliver is a critical role. Change management is a shared responsibility from the top of the organization to efforts at the grassroots level that target the employees whose working lives will be directly impacted by the project. The CIO is a primary driver of change, coordinating the efforts of C-level executives and monitoring the impact of change on the organization.

The CEO should serve as the "celebrity spokesperson" for any large change effort, showing support from the top of the organization, and spreading the word about the change effort across business and geographical units of the corporation. While this role is highly visible, the role of the CIO is more behind the scenes, ensuring change efforts at the line level are taking hold, and that a

EXECUTIVE SUMMARY (CONTINUED)

cadre of change agents is delivering a more targeted message at the line level.

The corporation has several levers available to it to influence adoption of change, from the positive (like compensation or promotion), to the negative levers (like threats of dismissal). These levers should be used in combination to make adapting to the new processes and tools the path of least resistance. Human nature dictates that people naturally prefer habit and ritual, and unless there are compelling reasons that appeal directly to an individual's self-interest, they will likely avoid changing the way they work.

C-Suite Conversations: Bridget Reiss and Kathy Allen, CIO and CFO of Millipore Corporation

Bridget Reiss is the vice president of information technology at Millipore Corporation, a leading provider of products and services that improve productivity in biopharmaceutical manufacturing and in clinical, analytical, and research laboratories. Bridget reports to the CFO of Millipore, Kathy Allen, both of whom discussed Millipore's IT organization and the relationship between a CIO and CFO.

The IT function at Millipore is focused on maintaining a high level of quality in their ongoing operations. "Our job is to provide information technology services that are as simple as possible for our employees to use," notes Bridget. "It's like the light switch on the wall. There's tremendous infrastructure in place to make the lights come on, but you never think about it. You just flip the switch and you know the lights will come on, right?" While this operational aspect of IT is expected, Bridget has also managed to increasingly shift IT's focus toward the strategic aspects of Millipore's business. A key element of this transition has involved the integration of selected staffing and strategic skills from various business units into her IT organization.

Explaining this combination of businesspeople and technologists, Bridget states: "In the past, we only had information technology specialists in the department. Over the last several years, we've hired a number of businesspeople to broaden our perspective and to better align our focus with Millipore's corporate strategy. In fact, one recent addition was a divisional Director of Sales—who would know better about servicing an internal customer than a person who is an expert at interactions with our external customers?" Part of this shift to a more strategic focus entails looking for ways to leverage Millipore's IT services as a product offering, providing external customers with visibility into Millipore's systems to enhance customer service and to create the potential for IT to help drive revenues for the company.

Continued success will require a new set of competencies in the IT organization, what Bridget refers to as "a whole different set of skills and muscles." She notes, "External customers have higher demands than the 'captive audience' of internal employees. While we view our internal customers as very important to us, at the end of the day they're colleagues on the same Millipore team—so they tend to be a little bit more understanding of an issue than we'd expect a paying customer to be." In the case of external customers, the quality and overall service level becomes much more challenging. "If the customer is calling at two o'clock in the morning on Sunday because our systems aren't working, they want to talk to an expert who can resolve their problem immediately. This requires a very different support structure than what we have today."

This transition of IT from strictly an internal service to one that is valued by existing and new customers holds appeal beyond the IT organization. Kathy Allen, Millipore's CFO, sees this as a logical progression, similar to the evolution of the supply chain. "It started with customers wanting their transactional interfaces to be highly automated," notes Kathy, "with simplicity, accuracy, and reliability that makes Millipore easy to do business with."

This automation, though highly valuable to customers, is not the whole story. "I think the next step involves leveraging and further extending the value of our application knowledge and expertise to our customers" says Kathy. IT is one more element of this differentiating next step.

Kathy and Bridget have a long history with Millipore and a personal working relationship that spans 20 years; their current reporting relationship as CFO and CIO has been in place for over five years. They defy the conventional wisdom that a CIO reporting to the CFO creates an IT department primarily focused on cost control and financial rigor. Kathy sees her role not as a budget watchdog, but as she puts it: "a partner around leveraging technology for the overall benefit of Millipore's business." Kathy sees process improvement as the cornerstone of the relationship between the CIO and CFO. "I think the relationship centers around a common goal of process improvement and ensuring that the organization is getting the data needed to make informed business decisions. For example, one of the highly successful IT initiatives entailed the implementation of an improved tool set for our field sales organization to give them better information to drive higher sales levels."

Bridget sees the reporting relationship between CIO and CFO in a similar positive light, commenting that, "in IT we consider ourselves to be fortunate to have Kathy as our spokesperson representing us and providing guidance. She's been in the trenches with us and she knows what it takes to implement information systems. This support is critical in helping to identify the resources and challenges around implementing IT systems and to focus our efforts on the strategic projects that have the biggest impact for our company." While the formal reporting relationship creates important support for the CIO, Millipore's matrix reporting structure provides Bridget with accessibility to other senior executives. "I've always felt that we can go to any of the senior people in the company and work hand in hand with them on initiatives we're trying to achieve for the corporation. It's about great execution and teamwork."

Kathy's role is also that of a "sounding board" for Bridget and the IT organization. Bridget describes this as "a soft-touch role with the people in the organization. The IT group sets high standards and they have tremendous respect for Kathy. Occasionally if we fall short of our standards, Kathy is always there to remind us of how often we have already succeeded, help us understand the lessons learned, and agree on a go-forward game plan. We generally walk away feeling reinvigorated and inspired. Given the complexity of many of these projects, having this inspiration and support is important since there will inevitably be times when these projects don't go exactly as planned. So you can see how her demeanor is so critical toward establishing a risk-taking culture and a learning organization."

Another interesting facet of the CIO and CFO relationship at Millipore is that it does not have the rigor around ROI that one might expect. Interestingly, Kathy sees detailed ROI on IT investments as somewhat of a "falsehood." Instead, Kathy looks at IT funding as an investment in the current and future operational efficiency of the corporation, much like an investment in manufacturing capacity and capability. "The key factor," continues Kathy, "is a matter of setting IT's priorities against the backdrop of the company's overall set of priorities. Naturally we have limits on our IT spending. Quite frankly, our challenge is one of prioritization, which all too often in IT is based on factors that transcend the classical ROI model." Prioritizing projects becomes more of a strategic discussion. Kathy explains this process: "Bridget leads the discussion on what she thinks are the right priorities. At the executive level of the company, we must agree that these are the right priorities for the IT organization before funding is allocated. While we do incorporate ROI analysis where possible, we do not set priorities on the strict basis of financial payback. At Millipore, it's more about mapping our IT investments to the overall strategic objectives of the corporation rather than taking a top-down scientific approach based solely on financial rigor."

Key to this process is the knowledge held in the IT organization and an ability to rapidly dismiss those projects that are completely outside the priorities of the corporation. Bridget explains that "there's a tremendous amount of experience here at Millipore. We capitalize on our know-how and execute on our commitments. That of course builds credibility for the future and good business partnerships."

This teamwork extends beyond Millipore's employees to vendor partnerships. Oracle has been a key partner with Millipore for over 17 years and their software serves as the core of Millipore's ERP software. "We have an excellent relationship with Oracle," notes

Bridget. "When you can achieve a pairing of vision and openness, the result is a mutual dependency to make things happen. Success becomes the norm."

Over the past three years, Millipore has been building a culture of taking calculated risks and asking the right questions should a decision lead to the wrong outcome. When asked how this culture has been fostered, Kathy explains that, "Millipore strives to differentiate between reckless risk taking and intelligent risk taking. As I mentioned earlier, one role of the IT organization is to make sure the organization is getting the data needed to make informed business decisions. When taking risks, I think we've largely been fortunate with the outcomes because up-front we identify risk symptoms, severities, contingencies, and mitigations. Remember, this is all about calculated risk; we are not about recklessness!" Millipore's role as a life sciences company inherently contributes to this culture of risk taking, but it is also a frequent topic at the executive level. Kathy says, "It needs to become more of a process and a learning activity as opposed to a subtlety within the culture, because it's not something we're consistently good at quite yet. But we're getting there—I've seen great progress and discipline over the past year. We believe we cannot drive exceptional revenue and profitability performance without taking calculated risks."

These attitudes toward risk taking and failure allow the executives at Millipore to readily admit those infrequent IT failures, determine what went wrong, and use that information to move the company forward. Kathy commented on Millipore's success at this process, noting the executive level's ability to speak to the employee population on a "hey-we-stopped-this-project-and-it's-okay-that-we-stopped-this-project" basis in those rare cases when it becomes apparent that the project will not accomplish the predetermined objectives.

The upbeat dynamic and obvious respect that Kathy and Bridget have for each other clearly demonstrates that a CIO who reports to the CFO of an organization is not at an immediate disadvantage, and that the working relationship easily trumps the reporting relationship. A critical aspect of that dynamic involves having a CFO who views IT as a strategic enabler. A focused IT organization can find an ally in the CFO, and use that to create a Breakthrough IT organization. As Kathy sees it: "It's a really great group of people, with strong leadership, and they act with very high standards. They really push themselves to the highest level of performance and you can see it in the quality of all the things they do."

CHAPTER 8

Cashing in the Chips
When to Cancel
a Project

One of the most difficult decisions an executive team must make is when an investment is no longer meeting its targets, and any associated resources should be allocated elsewhere. This is clearly the case with a financial instrument, and the pain of the decision is even more acute when dealing with strategic projects. Large commitments of money, personnel, and management oversight are required, and often careers and reputations are staked on the success of a large project. Like the gambler putting his or her last few chips into play and hoping for a miracle, we often throw more resources at a losing proposition rather than walking away from the table.

Of the many risks to strategic projects, not facing a cancellation decision head on and considering the option of canceling a project at the first signs of distress can cause far more damage to the organization than making a swift and momentarily painful decision. With so much on the line, how do you know when a project is hopeless versus a project that just needs one final push to overcome those last few roadblocks? This chapter examines these questions.

My Little Runaway

Most of us have heard stories in the business press of runaway projects, those well-intentioned endeavors that kept needing "just a little more" money or time. They gradually stretch out, requiring two, three, or more times their original budget and implementation time. Very rarely was the team comprised of complete incompetents, and often proven internal leaders, high-dollar implementation firms, and software or methodologies with an excellent track record were employed, but the results were nonetheless disastrous. Some delivered nothing but a slow burn of corporate resources, while others put key aspects of a company's business at risk, requiring expensive reactionary measures, and occasionally driving a corporation to the brink of ruin.

Risk is inherent in any task, especially something as complex as a strategic project that combines changes to systems, processes, and the way people work, but there are several ways to mitigate those risks. Many feel that top-dollar implementation help or proven software will make all the difference; however, these have become a basic assumption in the current business environment, rather than a differentiator and key for success. The primary means of preventing a runaway project, identifying it, and canceling it are:

- Controlling scope
- Setting failure criteria
- Managing cancellation

These three points seem very simple on paper, yet can be difficult to manage successfully, and are the basis for controlling the performance of your project and identifying when it is time to cancel.

The Project Killers

If you have spent any time around project management experts or any of the formal project management methodologies, you have likely heard of the "three levers": time, scope, and budget. The theory of the three levers suggests that you can control any two of the levers, but the third lever reacts on its own, and cannot be controlled. For example, you may tighten the timeline of the project, and hold the scope steady, which will cause a jump in the budget of the project, since you will likely need more resources and investment to complete the same amount of scope in a shorter period of time. This example is graphically depicted in Exhibit 8.1.

The Three Lever Theory continues with the assumption that if you can react to and monitor the three levers, you can keep your project from spiraling out of control, or at least have a preemptive warning that one of the levers will be increasing outside of your influence if two others are changing. Another classic example is if budget reductions are demanded, along with a shorter timeline, the scope must be reduced.

While the three levers look good on paper, and dovetail nicely with common sense, they make one critical flawed assumption when applied to strategic projects: that the scope and associated timeline are well defined and quantifiable at all times. If you know exactly the amount of work that is to be done, and the exact amount of time it takes to complete each piece of work, determining budget and monitoring

EXHIBIT 8.1

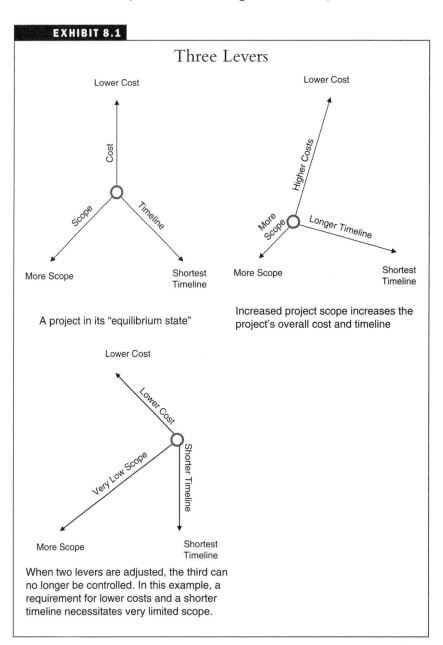

Three Levels

A project in its "equilibrium state"

Increased project scope increases the project's overall cost and timeline

When two levers are adjusted, the third can no longer be controlled. In this example, a requirement for lower costs and a shorter timeline necessitates very limited scope.

the three levers are fairly easy. In frequently repeated projects—for example, installing a new workstation or upgrading an application—the three levers can be applied with a fair amount of certainty. Plugging in a keyboard, or installing an application to a known number of workstations, are consistent from a three-levers perspective, whereas something like ensuring the sales force has adapted a new process is not.

One of the problems with applying the three levers to strategic projects is that a timeline and budget are often set in stone well before any detailed assessment of the scope has been made. As the team becomes bogged down in the details of the implementation, the scope begins to wildly expand and contract, and tasks that seemed simple now appear daunting, and vice versa. In addition, to continue building the credibility of IT as a strategic investment, expenditures for a particular project and the timeline for return on investment, which drives the overall project timeline, must be rigorously controlled. IT will never be viewed as a strategic investment in the C-suite if its investment costs and timelines are subject to wild fluctuations, making investing in strategic projects more of a crapshoot than a sound organizational investment strategy.

For the Breakthrough IT organization, the primary lever for controlling a project becomes scope. Budget and timeline serve as warning flags and diagnostic tools more than areas that should be constantly adjusted. They in turn feed ROI, which becomes the ultimate success indicator of the project. That said, scope is often an area many projects fail to control and jealously guard. Many projects leave the scope to junior resources, or create "wish lists" with thousands of disjointed items or features that a project team then struggles to implement, serving as passengers on a runaway train rather than conductors that ensure scoping decisions are primarily the province of the project team. Scope is also inexorably tied to time and budget, and indirectly is the only way to control these two areas. Letting scope run amuck or failing to ensure any scope change requests are carefully discussed and vetted is a recipe for trouble.

Should scope begin to blossom, or if the initial assessment of project scope inadequately captured the extent of a project's work, more detailed attention must be paid to the project, and its current state compared to a well-defined set of failure criteria.

Setting Failure Criteria

Organizational project management could do itself a favor by borrowing some concepts from engineering. Complex devices and machines are made vastly easier to maintain by taking a key decision away from those on the front lines: when a component has failed. Before a product is placed into production, tolerances and specifications for critical components are analyzed, and a failure point is determined in advance. Rather than a maintenance technician pondering if an aircraft engine can make another flight, that technician references the tolerances for a particular component, and if that component is outside of tolerance, it is exchanged or the plane does not fly. The decision is not made in the heat of battle, debated, and deliberated; rather, the tolerances are well known in advance, eliminating debate and questioning and making the decision on a failed component a binary one. The component is either within its tolerance or outside of it and must be replaced.

While this example seems simplistic, a major mistake in determining when to cancel a project occurs before the project has even

158

commenced, when the project selection committee and executive sponsors neglect to discuss failure criteria before the work begins. While it may seem somewhat morbid to discuss failure before you even begin work on a new task, the savings for the organization should failure happen are immense.

Advance planning of failure criteria also helps prevent attempts at last-minute heroics, and those painful decisions on whether "just a few more dollars" will make the difference in a struggling project. Corporate leaders, including the CEO and CIO, are also at their most objective before the project has begun. Little money has been spent, and careers have not yet been bet on the success of a particular initiative. Setting failure criteria at this point provides an objective benchmark that can be referenced as the company becomes fully invested in the daily work of driving the project to completion.

When the Going Gets Tough—Warning Signs

As mentioned in previous chapters, the key to measuring strategic projects in the Breakthrough IT organization is tracking their completion based on the ROI they have delivered, compared to the costs that have been expended. This classic cost-benefit analysis is far more meaningful when there is a stake in the ground, and failure criteria have been set in advance of the project. Even if existing projects have not had failure criteria set in advance of their commencing, it is a good idea to develop and document criteria any time a project passes a deadline or requires more money or resources, sure signs that something is not going according to plan.

Like any investment, thresholds must be established that reflect the company's tolerance for additional risk and additional costs. They should be reviewed and justified, and only broken for good reason. While it may seem like an additional layer of administrative overhead, a good time to evaluate the project against its failure criteria is any time a new resource is requested, be it additional staff or more money. Key questions that should be asked of each new request are:

- What piece of functionality or scope is requiring more resources (remember, scope is the only lever truly within our control)?
- Why is the resource needed? Do we need more resources for the same amount of scope due to a miscalculation during planning, or is the scope expanding and requiring more resources?

If one element of project scope is consistently requiring more resources, diagnostic and corrective action can be taken in that area. If many areas of the project are requiring additional, unplanned resources, there is a problem with the project as a whole, and an early indication that the project is in danger of failure. At this point, it is important to determine if the project is failing due to a poor understanding of the original scope or a poor job of estimating resource requirements. If the latter is the case, the simplest solution is to "pause" work on the project and validate all resource estimates before continuing the project in earnest. If the original estimates were wildly off-target, the selection committee of the PMO should reevaluate the project, since initial ROI and time estimates will likely have been incorrect. In this case, the rules of the game have changed, and blindly adding resources will likely result in a runaway project, or one that costs far more than the benefit it produces.

In the other case, where the addition of resources indicates a poor understanding of the project's scope, the project should immediately be paused, and the entire business case for the project reevaluated. Continuing a project in this state is like landing on the shores of an unknown continent with no map, and hoping to reach the other shore within a predefined timeline and a limited budget. While "boldly going where no man has gone before" makes for good science fiction, continuing a project after it becomes clear that the scope of the work is largely unknown is a recipe for disaster.

Broaching the Topic of Cancellation

No one likes to admit defeat, especially in the realm of strategic projects. These initiatives take months or even years to gain support and momentum, hundreds of hours of meetings and analysis to build a business case, and then months to ramp up and actually begin the work. Reputations and even careers may be at stake, making the topic of canceling a project, after all the work and investment in moving it forward, a difficult one.

There is a balance between being seen as an alarmist, who mentions cancellation at the slightest sign of trouble, and the brave soldier who falls on his or her sword, trying to push the project forward against all odds, and leaving a trail of wasted money and dysfunctional systems and processes in his or her wake. The balance between the two comes largely from again looking at the project though an investment lens. Monies spent on the project should be easy to ascertain, and timelines should be more accurate now that the project is in full swing than when it was originally proposed. At the simplest level, the current burn rate of the project can be extrapolated across the estimated number of days to completion, and cost to complete determined. While this is easy enough, it means little without being compared to the original scope and ROI estimates for the project.

Many projects have a tendency to reduce functionality or the breadth of the initiative as costs increase, and end up in a position where costs have doubled or tripled, while the ROI that will be garnered from the reduced scope has fallen dramatically—a one-two punch that destroys the value of a project at a far more aggressive pace than burn rate alone. Understanding how scope has changed, in addition to your burn rate, allows for an updated forecast of the project's ROI. If you follow the methods for managing projects mentioned in this book, this should be a fairly easy task, since each large piece of the project scope has a corresponding ROI associated with it.

As Exhibit 8.2 shows, once a project is faced with increasing costs combined with lowered scope, ROI diminishes at a rapidly accelerating rate, eventually turning negative. There is a very high risk that what is delivered will not match what was originally planned and accepted by the project selection committee.

Bringing the topic of project cancellation up for consideration is generally not taken lightly, yet with the pressure for success often clouding the better judgment of those directly tied to the project, this discussion usually happens too late rather than too early. As soon as a project begins to experience the dual pressures of increasing burn rate and decreasing ROI, it is a good time to consider cancellation. At the end of the day, any project that will not generate acceptable ROI based

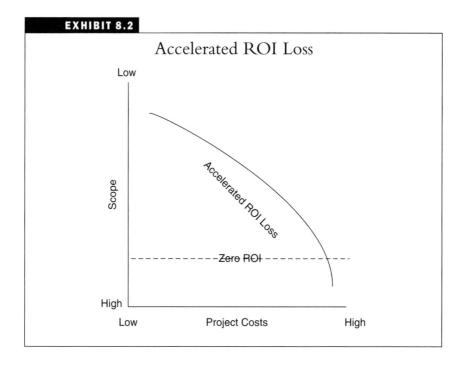

EXHIBIT 8.2

Accelerated ROI Loss

on the estimated costs to complete the project should be cancelled. The methodology discussed in Chapter 1 should be applied to the project in its current state, assigning an ROI estimate to each of the major components of scope that are remaining. At this point, current burn rate should be easily determined, and estimates based on the remaining scope can be formulated. With these figures in hand, there should be a clear business case for canceling the project based on the decreasing ROI. Cancellation need not be a complete and total admission of failure, however, as a central component of the analysis completed to support or defer cancellation is the cost to complete the project. Canceling when the time is right could save a significant amount of money and free the organization to pursue other opportunities, rather than pouring cash into a failing project with no end in sight.

Canceling Well

A similar process to one that initiated the project should occur when making the final decision to cancel. A defined group of executives, similar to the project selection committee, should have the ultimate vote in determining if the project should be cancelled. Facts should be investigated, the keys being the current estimated ROI of the project, and the estimated cost needed to achieve that ROI. Once again, the current level of risk of the project should be considered. If the project has gone from low risk and the associated low returns to significant risk, with even lower returns, the decision to cancel should be straightforward.

Once a cancellation decision is made, the real work of canceling a project well begins. Often, once a project is cancelled, those associated with the project allow human nature to take over, and attempt to distance themselves from the project as rapidly as possible. In their zeal to rid themselves of the project and eliminate its ongoing costs, many companies pack up the project team and abandon anything of value that was generated during the course of the project.

The most valuable resource of even the most dramatic project failure is the staff that participated on the project team. The Breakthrough IT organization cannot allow a failed project to serve as a mark against staff that participated in the project without legitimate reason. When projects begin, often volunteers are solicited, or top performers from various business units are recruited for the project team. After several months on a project, their old positions are often filled, and should a project be cancelled, they are often left in the lurch, legitimately fearing for their jobs. One of the first tasks in canceling a project well is initiating an HR effort to ensure the highest-performing members of the project team do not fall through the cracks and end up being dismissed. Providing these assurances and making a highly visible effort to rank and rate each member of the project team identifies a pool of high-quality resources available for other positions, and reduces the uncertainty of the project team. People who are concerned for their jobs are likely not going to apply themselves to the work of capturing any value that was generated by the cancelled project, compounding the financial loss the project represents.

The HR process during project cancellation should also seek to recognize any new skills or advancement each person on the project team achieved. While the project as a whole may not have been successful, often individuals will excel in a difficult project environment, and learn new skills that may be useful in other areas of the organization. Once employees are assured that presence on a failed project alone will not derail their career, ensure that they are evaluated by whoever managed them during the project, be it an internal manager or an external consultant.

Once an HR process is in place, canceling the project should be treated as a mini-project in itself, and if your project management office is hitting its stride, it should have templates detailing shutdown tasks and a method for capturing whatever value was generated by the project. Items your project may have generated that should be investigated and captured include:

- Documentation of existing processes, which can be used for process reengineering efforts or future operational documentation

- New process designs, which can be considered for full or partial implementation as a separate project

- Organizational diagrams detailing current management and reporting structures, and any plans for new organizational designs

- New forms, documentation standards, or project management processes the PMO can capture and use on future projects

- New talent in management and process analysis that can be used on other projects or back in a business unit

Any of the aforementioned items may be complete to a point where it could feed into another project, or be the basis of a smaller project. If nothing else, most strategic projects produce detailed process documentation about how an element of the business currently functions. This documentation can be reviewed and the documented process improved, even if a systems component or integration with a larger project will be abandoned. If nothing else, this type of documentation can be invaluable in producing operational manuals and training materials. If a similar project is initiated in the future, accurate documentation of existing processes can save months of analysis work, and serve as a starting point for another effort. Too often, this type of documentation is left in a dusty archive, never to be used again although a significant amount of time and money was expended in its production.

In addition to capturing whatever value was produced before the project was cancelled, an effort to conduct a "post mortem" on the project can provide valuable insight into what caused the project to fail. When conducting this analysis, look for answers to the following questions:

- Were the original ROI estimates correct? Were they too aggressive? Why?

- Was the scope of the project detailed and correct, or were several problems uncovered during the course of the project?

- Was the right leadership team in place, from the CIO down to project managers and team leaders? Were the right people participating in the project?

- Was this project seen as just another IT project, or was there an understood business benefit, and were business unit resources fully invested in the project?

- Was there some significant unforeseen cost? Did a particular part of the project require far more resources than originally anticipated, indicating a possible problem with the scope estimates?

- Was decision making crisp and efficient, or did the project waste a significant amount of time waiting for decisions that were subject to constant revision?

- Were any technologies used by the project difficult to implement, or not up to the task?

- Did an unforeseen change occur in the external environment, such as a broad economic or competitive change? If the environment changes again, should the project be restarted?

This list may serve as a starting point for your organization's own detailed list of postmortem questions. Aside from capturing any completed work from the project, ascertaining what went wrong from an operational, tactical, and strategic perspective is the most valuable exercise that can be done to gain some value from a failed project. Looking at a failed project from those perspectives, and avoiding the urge to assign blame to particular individuals or business units, can be a massive insurance policy on the success of future efforts. Determining that a project failed due to having the wrong resources and attempting to implement an immature technology makes future projects in a similar area easier, since these caveats are known in advance and can be built into the project before it even begins.

Closing Time

With an HR process in place, capturing each individual's achievements and coaching points, and a "mini-project" in full swing to capture any value produced by the project and determine areas that contributed to the project's failure, the time comes to officially terminate the project. During the closing process, HR should be shopping for positions for the highest performers on the project, looking to other projects or business unit positions. Failed projects can be a grueling test of a manager's ability, and the best leaders should shine through in difficult times and be rewarded and redeployed appropriately.

Implementation partners will often be scrambling once a cancellation is announced, attempting to shop their own people and move them to a longer-term engagement immediately. While quickly dismissing external resources to cut costs is tempting, ensure any special knowledge or processes they have developed have been captured and documented. Project managers should facilitate sessions to detail each person's unique areas of responsibility, and ensure they are captured before leaving the project through a formal checklist process. Knowledge transfer is often a selling point of the large implementation companies, yet it is the responsibility of the company writing the checks to ensure that this process is actually completed, especially when the implementation company is under pressure to redeploy its resources as quickly as possible.

There are many mundane logistical aspects to closing a project as well, which should be executed in parallel with the project closure process, from returning equipment used by implementation partners to tracking which offices are free with facilities. With the team rapidly diminishing and all articles of value captured, the final task is to inform the organization that the project has been cancelled and give an overview of the reasons from an investment perspective. Once again, there is a temptation to bury the cancellation under the proverbial rug, engendering conversations years after the project was terminated wondering whatever happened to Project X. While admitting failure is not a task many relish, informing the organization that the project is cancelled and providing an overview of why lends credibility to the IT organization. This communication also allows the company to move forward, acknowledging the failure and the lessons learned, and moving the project off the company radar, ending speculation and concern over its fate.

Canceling a project should always be an investment decision, not an indictment of the organization or its leaders and those responsible for the daily operations of the project. Even the most painful cancellations generally have delivered something of value that can be used by the organization or fed into another effort, and if the reasons for the project's failure are analyzed, understood, and acted upon, the cancellation will likely improve the performance of future efforts. Avoiding the temptation to lay blame, and "jump ship" from the project before anything of value can be captured, and acknowledging and informing the organization about the failure allows the Breakthrough IT organization to rapidly abandon failing efforts, and move resources to the next strategic project.

ACTION POINTS

Action points provide concrete steps you can use to begin implementing ideas from this chapter. For this chapter, the action points are:

- Determine failure criteria for any projects that are currently underway. Failure criteria should include metrics like maximum spend, ROI variance, and scope variance. Monitor struggling projects closely in relation to these failure criteria.

- Ensure the PMO has a project postmortem checklist in place. This checklist should be designed to help ascertain why a cancelled project failed, and captures any lessons that will help avoid future project failures.

- Develop a relationship with Human Resources, and discuss a process for identifying high-performing staff and integrating them back into the organization or staffing them on another project, should their current project be cancelled. Ensure that every project has strong HR involvement to ensure experiences, new skills, and employee development are adequately documented and managed.

- Develop "rolloff checklists" for implementation partner staff. Too often, knowledge transfer happens only when the company writing the checks forces it.

- Analyze several past projects that were cancelled using the newly developed postmortem toolkit. This process should

ACTION POINTS (CONTINUED)

determine the effectiveness of the toolkit, and develop your project execution expertise by analyzing past cancellations.

- Determine if past projects were cancelled later than they could have been, and what reasons led to delaying the cancellation decision.

 EXECUTIVE SUMMARY

Canceling a failing strategic project is a task that is rarely done well. Large amounts of time and money are at stake, not to mention reputations and sometimes careers bet on the success of the effort. When a decision is made to cancel a project, too often those involved with the effort attempt to distance themselves from the failure as quickly as possible, fearing a negative mark on their careers.

The key to understanding when to cancel a project is a grasp on what factors the project team can control, and what indicators correspond to those factors that can be tracked to determine the status of the project. Perhaps the only item directly under the control of a project team is the scope of the project. Scope dictates the time and cost of completing a project, and drives the expected financial returns the project will generate. If those returns begin to diminish as a project drags on, and scope is reduced to compensate, ROI is diminished at a rapidly increasing rate. Monitoring the expected ROI in relation to the project's ongoing costs gives the first indications that a project will not live up to its business case, and as the cost to complete the project increases, and ROI decreases, a failure point at which the project should be cancelled must be determined. This final "stake in the ground" helps move a cancellation decision from one of impassioned opinions to one based on the company's investment strategy. Canceling too late should be seen as a bad investment to be avoided, rather than corporate heroics of making a dramatic last stand when success is all but impossible.

Once a cancellation decision is made based on the project's potential ROI no longer being acceptable to the business, care must be taken to retrieve anything of value the project may have generated, and to institute an HR process to track and redeploy high performers on the project to other efforts or back into a business unit. In the zeal to abandon a failed effort, these tasks are often ignored at the organization's peril. An investigation into why the project failed should also be conducted, determining any "lessons learned" that might be applicable to other current or future strategic projects.

No matter how difficult a project has become, there is always some level of valuable work generated that can be captured, new talent developed, and lessons that can be applied to a future project. Canceling a project well is a central skill to the Breakthrough IT organization. Just as investment decisions do not always provide their expected payoffs, strategic projects sometimes fail. Deriving value even from failure separates the Breakthrough IT organization from those that flee failure, only to continually make the same mistakes in the future.

CHAPTER 9

Be Superman (or Wonder Woman) Coming in Late to a Struggling Shop

C oming into a new C-level position is a daunting endeavor, especially when a struggling IT organization is placed in your care. From the CEO's perspective, a floundering IT shop is a drag on the income statement, and if the other C-level executives are accustomed to an IT organization that functions quietly as a utility or shared service, changing the leadership is often an effort to end the "noise" coming from what is perceived as a utility business function that should not produce any distractions.

The first several weeks of a new CIO's tenure are a critical period. The new CIO has an advantage in being a fresh face, both in terms of having an outsider's view of the organization and its IT shop, and being expected to make some changes. It is assumed that the new leader will "shake things up," and there is no better time than early in his or her tenure. The first several weeks also serve as a critical period of relationship building. Any biases, assumptions, or past history associated with the former CIO are no longer in consideration, and the new CIO can start fresh. This also means that the former CIO's successes are quickly forgotten, and that the new CIO will face intense scrutiny on his or her first few steps in the new position.

While much of this book assumes a gradual change from a focus on ongoing operations to executing business strategy, the new CIO is often faced with many operational challenges upon his or her arrival in a new company, or after landing in the top IT job at his or her current company. Operations and "fire fighting" are going to be the primary responsibilities during the first month in the position, and the march toward Breakthrough status will likely take a backseat during this time.

Arriving on the Scene

The first task of the new CIO is stabilizing the current operating environment. If the former CIO left the position under duress, focusing on stabilizing IT operations is likely going to be a full-time job for months rather than weeks. If the IT shop was run as a utility and the CIO was the primary decision maker on how to respond to any catastrophe no matter how big or small, ongoing operations will also occupy a large percentage of the new CIO's time. Stabilizing the IT environment consists of three major areas:

1. Identify current operational problems. These are the areas in which IT is spending most of its time in reactionary mode, be they

systems, projects, or "externally forced" problems like hacker attacks or failing infrastructure.

2. Determine the IT organization's capabilities in terms of human resources, budget, and how focused your staff are on technical skills versus more general business process expertise.

3. Transition ongoing operations to a trusted group of managers, so the focus of the CIO can shift to building relationships within the C-suite and larger business community, and optimization of the organization's project portfolio can begin.

Fixing the Cracks: Stabilizing Operations

C-suite colleagues are usually willing to give the new CIO the benefit of the doubt as that person reshapes the IT organization as he or she sees fit. However, there will be little of the same flexibility when problems crop up that require an immediate reaction. Soon after you have settled into your new office and discovered the location of the nearest coffeemaker, "firefighting" will begin. Most managers assume new leaders will want to make major decisions themselves, or at the very least hear about each and every problem, so the new CIO is likely to be deluged with questions and notified of every issue after arriving on the scene.

As attractive as jumping right into each problem and attempting to heroically present a solution in the nick of time might seem, this approach will likely lead to long hours and increasing frustration. Before attempting to discover solutions, it is critical that the new CIO size up current operational problems, classify them as requiring an immediate, short, or long-term solution, assigning a priority to each and then building a team to implement a solution. While these immediate concerns are not necessarily strategic projects, many of the techniques for managing strategic projects and determining and tracking the ROI associated with each are applicable to this process, albeit on a smaller scale.

A mistake that is easy to make when assuming the CIO role is awarding each problem the same priority, or making the highest-priority problem the one that was most recently discovered. The "problem portfolio" should be managed like the portfolio of strategic projects, and the IT organization's limited resources allocated toward fixing problems that will have the highest value to the corporation first. Each new issue should be vetted against the master list, and just because it is a new problem, or one that is of particular importance to one business unit, IT should not chase each flavor of the day.

This process of identifying problems and determining their priority is completed with far less rigor and formality than would be associated with strategic projects, and the ultimate goal of the CIO should be to assemble ad hoc teams around each problem that drive toward a solution and report progress to the CIO, rather than the CIO becoming personally involved in each and every decision. This serves two purposes, the obvious one being that it frees the CIO to determine the competency of his or her organization and begin setting the stage for a move toward Breakthrough status.

The subtler, and perhaps more important purpose for transferring daily responsibility for finding a solution to each of these problems is getting a grasp on the competency of the CIO's immediate subordinates. Managing a small team around a minor problem is an excellent way to vet future leaders of strategic projects in a lower-risk environment. If a particular manager is not up to the task, he or she can be quickly replaced with minimal risk to finding a solution to the problem at hand. This use of ad-hoc teams also tests the IT organization's ability to manage a process, and interact with its counterparts in other business units. This process gives the CIO a view into how well the IT organization functions within the context of the corporation at large. Are the members of that organization competent? Are they well respected and capable of finding a solution to a problem and executing on delivering that solution? This use of ad-hoc teams immediately demonstrates the capabilities of the IT organization to the CIO, making up for the years of observation and fine-tuning that were available to their predecessor in a short time.

Finding the Source: What Kind of IT Operation Have You Inherited?

As your ad-hoc teams built around current pressing problems begin to make progress, it is a good time to begin looking at the focus of IT in terms of what percentage of IT money and mindshare are expended on operations versus executing business strategy. A shift to Breakthrough status generally occurs when the CIO spends about 60 percent of his or her time focusing on executing business strategy, and less than 40 percent on ongoing operations. While operational issues should be the primary concern of a new CIO, once teams are in place to tackle pressing operational issues, the CIO should shift toward developing a plan for shifting the IT organization to Breakthrough status as soon as possible.

Begin by investigating how the IT organization spends most of its time. Chapter 1 provides an overview of engineering and utility-based IT functions, and most troubled IT organizations fall somewhere between the two. Depending on the circumstances of the previous CIO's departure, your IT shop may even combine an engineering or utility focus with being stuck in a completely operational mode, focused on solving problems as they are reported, with little or no focus on how IT can be a strategic asset to the business. As expressed in the previous section, this reactionary mode must be fixed before all else, or any attempt at moving IT into a strategic role will be met with failure.

With a determination made as to how the IT shop's focus is divided between ongoing operations and the execution of strategic projects, a look at sourcing ongoing operations should begin. Start by investigating the various activities that are candidates for a sourcing change immediately after getting a process in place to track and manage immediate problems. It is best not to institute a sourcing change until these teams begin to deliver results and IT is no longer in a completely reactionary mode. Sourcing changes are mini-projects in themselves, and attempting to change the way IT does business while reacting to myriad problems and issues will create conflicting demands for the organization's focus, and neither process will be completed well.

Successfully managing the barrage of initial issues will also identify immediate subordinates who can help manage the change in sourcing, and in the case of insourcing, may be viable candidates for leading an internal organization dedicated to a particular IT function. Sourcing changes usually have associated cost reductions, which will please colleagues in the C-suite, who generally look to a new CIO to bring about business change and a more efficient cost structure. The same considerations presented in early chapters for making a decision between insourcing and outsourcing will be present when a new CIO begins his or her tenure; however, a bias toward insourcing may be the best way to proceed depending on the political sensitivity and the size of the organization or function that will experience the sourcing change.

With immediate problems recognized, prioritized, and handed off to ad-hoc teams, and sourcing options developed and sourcing transitions underway, the CIO can make a more thorough investigation of the capabilities of the IT organization.

Who Works for You?

In addition to the problems, cost structures, and emotional baggage related to IT that the new CIO inherits, that person also finds him- or herself surrounded by people who were hired on another's watch. This may be a very beneficial fact, if the previous CIO staffed the organization well. Subordinates may have longstanding relationships with their peers in other business units, and may have built high-performing teams that are respected throughout the organization. However, there may be subordinates who felt they deserved IT's top job far more than you, and will do everything within their power to sabotage your first few weeks on the job. With the most pressing problems facing IT acknowledged, tracked, and handed off to a series of ad-hoc teams, the CIO should turn his or her attention to those who work for him or her.

The reactionary mode IT usually finds itself in upon the arrival of a new CIO is the perfect time to evaluate the people who make up the ranks of the IT organization, with close attention paid to the CIO's immediate subordinates, and a general evaluation of the rank and file. Immediate critics of the new CIO, those who were passed for the position or still remain loyal to your predecessor, must be identified immediately, and a working relationship established. If that fails, dismissing an ardent critic may be the best course of action, especially if that person's criticism translates into poor performance and attempts to derail the performance of the new CIO become apparent.

Observing subordinates' performances on the teams that are assembled to solve any immediate problems should serve as a "trial by fire" and allow the new CIO to determine the capabilities of each. Pay particular attention to each person's ability to independently manage the tasks he or she is assigned, and try to determine which people are excellent operational managers who can drive a task to completion, versus those who are strategists or tacticians, who spend more time planning the attack and tend to shy away from execution. Most problems faced by IT will involve some interaction with other business units, and if the CIO is to strive for Breakthrough status, these interactions will be a key test of IT's ability to relate to other business units. This interaction will determine whether IT will be seen as a strategic partner rather than an engineering group or utility function that has no place in executing business strategy. The CIO should surround him- or herself with people from each group, including:

Relationship builders: Those who can interact with their colleagues outside IT as peers, and are respected for their business and process knowledge, rather than technical acumen.

Strategists/tacticians: Subordinates who can take a complex problem and develop a strategy for finding its solution. These people can quickly grasp how the problem at hand fits in with the larger business environment, and chart a solution that will maximize the value to the organization as a whole.

Executors: Executors quickly go from a high-level solution to assembling the people and resources required to solve a problem, mapping the detailed steps of determining and deploying a solution to the correct people. Not just a project manager, the executor generates the plan *and* gathers and manages the resources required to deploy a solution.

As would be expected with any high-level position, some element of the relationship builder should be present in each of the three, especially in a Breakthrough IT organization in which interaction with other business units is a cornerstone of the organization. Ideally, key personnel should exemplify two of these criteria if not all three.

Line employees should be collectively evaluated based on the aforementioned roles, and in addition, some sense of their process competence versus their technical competence should be investigated. The best place to start this research is taking a sample of resumes of recent hires. Do they emphasize a particular technology and is their experience highly biased toward technology, or do they have a more general business process background? Chapter 4 details some of the criteria to look for in hiring employees for the Breakthrough IT organization, and these same criteria can be applied "retroactively" to determine where current employees stand on the spectrum of technical versus process competence. These two areas need not be mutually exclusive; however, technical competence can usually be bought as a commodity through temporary or consulting resources, while intimate knowledge of an organization's processes and the associated relationships between business units is far more difficult to acquire.

This analysis of the organization serves to identify people in the group who can immediately fill critical subordinate roles to the new CIO, and provide a picture of the larger IT organization and whether it has the necessary personnel to make the move to Breakthrough status. Recall that the Breakthrough IT organization is comprised primarily of process experts and change agents, both accustomed to working in a project environment rather than an operational role. If your current staff is far from that mark, the first few months of the new CIO's tenure are a perfect time to consider adjusting the organization's composition. The new CIO is expected to make HR changes, and at a minimum, he or she should ensure immediate subordinates exemplify the criteria required to build the Breakthrough IT organization. In addition, these subordinates should be empowered to make similar personnel changes within their teams to achieve the right mix of people.

While attacking any current problems, investigating potential ongoing operational processes, and shaking up the ranks of the IT organization may seem like a lot to tackle, and a significant series of changes to make in a short time span, rapid change and short-term pain usually create more long-term stability than working in an environment that is under a constant, gradual state of flux. Change is also expected of a new leader, and in the case of a struggling IT organization, dramatic change signals that the "bad old days" have run their course, and new leadership is taking every step necessary to improve the organization.

Tackling the Project Portfolio

Stabilizing the IT organization upon the arrival of the new CIO is an iterative process, and may take several months. As IT begins to transition from a reactive mode, the time comes to start investigating the organization's project portfolio. Similar to the employees of the IT organization, the project portfolio will be heavily shaped by the former CIO. He or she may have focused on a particular area of the business, or a certain software package. Regardless of the former CIO's strategy, existing projects should be investigated; their estimated ROI, return horizon, and risk determined; and current projects allocated in the risk/return matrix in Exhibit 9.1 and in Chapter 5.

Look for an overweighting or underweighting of a particular area, and investigate whether there are projects that are duplicating efforts that can be consolidated, or whether some change can be made to the

EXHIBIT 9.1

Project Portfolio Allocation Model			
Allocation	**Risk**	**Return Timeframe**	**Description**
30%	Low	Short	Quick fix
		Medium	
		Long	Infrastructure and maintenance
60%	Medium	Short	"Bread and butter" projects:
		Medium	process fixes, new tools, etc.
		Long	Foundational (ERP, CRM, etc.)
10%	High	Short	Reactionary
		Medium	Experimental
		Long	R&D

scope of an existing project to change your portfolio's allocation. Ensure that the business case for each project correctly represents the project in its current state as this may affect your allocation, and serves as a warning sign for any projects that have strayed far from their original business case and may be in danger of failing or not delivering anticipated results. Although a project may have begun on another's watch, the new CIO will likely be held accountable for the results, and therefore must pay particular attention to how each project is performing even if he or she would have done the project in a different manner, or not started it in the first place.

A complete shakeup of the current project portfolio can be a risky affair. Projects generally take months of analysis and debate to come to life, and unless there are no obvious impediments to success, scrapping a project with high organizational support is generally not the best course of action, even if it does not dovetail with the new CIO's vision of how the organization's project portfolio should be allocated. The new CIO should first ensure that current projects are meeting their stated objectives, and transition their status reporting and monitoring to an RIO basis as described in Chapter 6. As the position in the risk/ return matrix in Exhibit 9.1 becomes increasingly clear, scope can be modified or new projects added to the project portfolio to change the allocation mix to one that dovetails with the overall corporate strategy.

Another key dimension to look at when analyzing the organization's current project portfolio is whether the projects are truly strategic projects that involve business process change and the application of technology. Pure infrastructure projects are the hallmark of the engineering- and utility-based IT shops, and will lead to increased cost scrutiny, as IT is tasked with providing a commodity service rather than true organizational value. As operational processes are sourced to internal or external organizations, these infrastructure projects may also be transitioned or managed independently of true strategic projects. Pure infrastructure projects will never have the impact on business value that a strategic project brings, and they must be deemphasized as the IT organization makes the transition to Breakthrough status under the watch of the new CIO.

Turning the Wheel: Making the Leap to Breakthrough IT

Installing a new CIO and watching that person transition IT to Breakthrough status is a painstaking and iterative process. Much like reversing the direction of a long freight train, old behaviors must be slowed to a stop before a gradual acceleration in the opposite direction can begin. The benefits of Breakthrough IT should be fairly obvious to C-suite executives, and a lack of business value from an engineering- or utility-based IT shop may be one of the primary reasons for replacing the CIO in the first place. While the CEO or CFO may not articulate this as Breakthrough IT, too many executives have grown frustrated with IT shops that constantly consume cash and have little quantifiable value to show for it, eventually becoming like death or taxes: a necessary evil that will never go away. In this mode, there may not be anything "wrong" with IT other than the sense that it should be a source of competitive advantage rather than just a cost of doing business.

In the case of a new CIO, conversations around Breakthrough IT can be initiated by either the CIO or his or her boss, and an eye toward achieving Breakthrough status should drive the criteria for potential CIO candidates or be a cornerstone of the potential CIO's philosophy. Either way, the relationship between the CIO and his or her C-level colleagues is the key lever for building support for Breakthrough IT, and a critical channel for explaining the differences in how a Breakthrough IT organization is managed and evaluated, especially if the company is accustomed to a passive, utility-like IT function.

The new CIO is also likely to be observed more closely than a veteran whose style and philosophy are well known. The transition of ongoing operations may be surprising to some executives, and communication and relationship building becomes all the more critical to ensure the CEO and CFO understand the benefit of these changes, and the short- and long-term impact to the organization.

This transitional time, however, is also the best time to initiate fundamental changes to the IT organization. Responding to current pressing problems, investigating options for transitioning ongoing operations, and beginning to modify the personnel mix and project portfolio are highly visible initiatives that will move the IT organization toward Breakthrough status. As these dramatic changes begin to take effect, the CIO and CEO can work together on subtler changes, tweaking the project portfolio to dovetail more closely with corporate strategy, and building a PMO that can vet and track these projects and ensure they continue to deliver measurable monetary returns.

Many of the strategies around migrating to Breakthrough IT are applicable to the CIO who lands in a struggling shop, save for the initial focus on stabilizing operations. While this reactionary method of managing a business is not generally applicable to a Breakthrough IT shop, the metaphorical freight train must be slowed and stopped before its direction can be reversed.

Action points provide concrete steps you can use to begin implementing ideas from this chapter. For this chapter, the action points are:

- For the CEO considering new CIO candidates, base your selection criteria around Breakthrough IT. Do the candidates see IT as a potential value engine for the corporation? Do they have strong interpersonal skills that will allow them to relate and work closely with other members of the C-suite? Are they excellent business executives first, and technologists second?

- For potential CIOs, make Breakthrough IT one of your selling points when seeking the top IT job. Demonstrate that you are a business leader and capable potential colleague to the other C-suite executives. Show that above all else, you are willing and capable to use IT to execute the company's strategic direction, not merely play a sideline role maintaining infrastructure and pitching the latest system or product as a business "solution."

- For the CIO who has newly arrived at a troubled company, immediately get a grasp on current problems facing the IT organization, and triage each to determine the most critical. Resist the urge to tackle problems as they appear; rather, seek to prioritize and build a team to seek a solution as appropriate. Manage each problem as if it were a mini-project, tracking the status and ROI in a portfolio format that looks at pressing problems as a whole, rather than discrete units.

- Discuss the benefits of Breakthrough IT with C-suite colleagues. Arriving in a new position is the best time to implement change, since some level of turbulence is assumed with the arrival of a new leader. There is a balance between attempting to change too much, and missing this window of opportunity, but the best course of action is to get the people, relationships, and strategic project focus in place, even if it means dramatic change.

- Review the chapters of this book that are relevant to each stage of implementing Breakthrough IT as the need arises. Key chapters are the discussion of continuing operations and sourcing options in Chapter 2, relationship building among the C-suite in Chapter 3, assembling the right team in Chapter 4, and creating and managing the IT project portfolio in Chapters 5 and 6.

- Ensure the CIO has the right people as direct reports. The early stages of triage management can help demonstrate each subordinate's capabilities, and help determine who should fill critical positions moving forward. Investigate the IT organization as a whole, and determine whether personnel have the process focus and business knowledge to be able to relate to their business unit colleagues, or whether past hiring practices strongly favored technical competence above all else.

EXECUTIVE SUMMARY

Taking over the reins of a struggling IT shop is a challenge to any business leader; however, there is one distinct advantage to installing new leadership: an expectation of change. The newly installed CIO usually must react to a slew of problems the moment he or she arrives, legitimately forcing that person into a reactive mode of management at the onset of his or her CIO tenure. This is expected; however, each problem should be managed as a "mini-project," with a rapid analysis process conducted to determine the

EXECUTIVE SUMMARY (CONTINUED)

priority, impact, and potential financial return of each problem. Ad-hoc teams should be assembled to tackle each, which frees the CIO's attention span and allows the capabilities of his or her subordinates to be tested and evaluated on the job.

Any new leader is expected to bring about change in the organization he or she inherits, and the new CIO should be no exception. Many struggling IT shops are stuck in a reactive mode, or a focus on becoming an engineering or utility function has created an uncompetitive cost structure the new CIO is expected to rectify. Once immediate problems are under control, the first several weeks of the new CIO's career are the perfect time for discussions of the benefits of Breakthrough IT. Many eyes will be on the CIO, and there is usually a willingness to try new management styles. The CIO should present the case for Breakthrough IT as both a cost savings and value generation tool.

This is also a perfect time to shake up IT staff. The ad-hoc teams commissioned to solve pressing problems should be a test of leadership for immediate subordinates, and a more general analysis of hiring practices and current staff can help determine whether IT's personnel have what it takes to build a Breakthrough IT shop. A mix of process competence, change management, and project experience, and a solid relationship with business unit peers, should be preferred over pure technical competence.

With immediate problems under control, relationships with the C-suite and business unit leaders established, and IT staff transitioning to a cadre of process experts, the real work of Breakthrough IT can begin. The CIO can investigate sourcing options for ongoing operations, and dig into the organization's project portfolio, shifting the balance of projects to ensure it meets the company's strategic and tactical goals in the short and long terms.

C-Suite Conversations: Phil Stunt, Vice President, IT International, CA

Phil Stunt is the vice president, of IT International of CA (formerly Computer Associates). Phil is responsible for the IT operations of CA outside North America, his geographic areas of responsibility covering Europe, South America, Africa, and Asia, which account for nearly 50 percent of CA's sales. Phil works from CA's office in the United Kingdom, located outside London.

CA has been striving toward Breakthrough status in its IT organization. When asked where they are in that process, Phil commented, "If you look at what we preach, it is absolutely the Breakthrough IT–type scenario. If you look at where IT is positioned, I would say it is halfway there." While IT traditionally has been tasked with maintaining, as Phil puts it, the "boxes and wires," he sees IT moving toward a more strategic role. "We are being positioned as being one of the key drivers for the transformation of the business, and elements of it are starting to be seen as key enablers for market growth, geographic growth—whatever kind of growth it is."

Phil sees the CIO's reporting relationship as a key indicator of where IT is on the evolution to Breakthrough status. "I think a lot is guided by who the CIO reports to," he said. "If the CIO is still reporting into the CFO, then that is symptomatic or representative of the positioning of IT within that organization. If the CIO reports directly to the CEO, you would have to say that the organization and CEO see the IT organization as a key function—a key enabler—for his business. We are halfway: We report to the COO. Clearly, a major player but not yet a trusted advisor to the CEO-type role."

CA has been undergoing a massive transformation, both within IT from a systems and organizational perspective, and to the company as a whole. Phil sees this transformation as requiring every function within the corporation. "I hate the term 'the business' and IT. Who the hell is 'the business?' Well, guess what? I am 'the business.' We have to square that away in our own heads that it is not 'the business' or IT—we are all part of this thing called 'the business.'"

With the right mindset in place, Phil sees a measurable and proven delivery capability as the key to demonstrating the strategic value of the IT organization. "IT organizations generally have been very poor at showing and counting the value they have really delivered," said Phil. "We talk a lot about benefits realization; every project that I have ever been on or ever seen, benefits realization is a key part of the project. It is incredibly poorly executed by most organizations. Unless you can say 'Our business grew by X' or 'We shaved Y off the bottom line by doing this work that we drove from IT,' it is hard to say, 'By the way, I deserve a place at the top table.'"

This task of quantifying the value IT produces has been an ongoing struggle for Phil, especially since IT is generally regarded as taking a structured and rigorous approach to most tasks. "We usually have very good program managers and project managers because we have that structural approach in the way we think and do things," said Phil. When asked where this failure comes from, he commented: "That is because we retreat back into our shell of thinking around 'Yeah, what we do is we do the code and the business does the rest.' It is not true: You are implementing a change to the way you do business." This failing seems widespread, with Phil commenting that he has yet to see a company that does this well.

Outsourcing has changed the way a CIO looks at his or her operations. Phil sees two keys to achieving the maximum benefit from outsourcing: understanding your cost levels and creating portable processes. Regarding the former, Phil said, "One of the things you need to understand is: Are you actually at the right cost level for the organization and service you are trying to deliver?" The latter, perhaps more interesting point starts with an understanding of where to put your resources. "For Europeans, it used to be Dublin and then it was Prague and now it is India," said Phil. "Where next? Vietnam? Wherever the constant is today, isn't going to be a constant tomorrow. Companies are looking at Vietnam now very interestingly. India is becoming a more difficult place to put things because of the wage inflation." These shifts in the best locations to place resources drive the need for simple and portable processes. "It is just a natural sort of progression that happens. You need to have most of your basic infrastructure and the way you are operating fairly simple so you can adapt and change and be flexible as geographic advantages change," notes Phil. "You can get that flexibility only if you have a simplicity about your operations. If it is complex it is very difficult to change; it is very difficult to move." When asked how to plan for these shifting costs and preferred locations, Phil said: "In my head, I can't predict where the next great offshore, inshore opportunity will be but I need to think about how can I make sure that my operation is simplified enough to allow me to take advantage of that as and when it becomes apparent."

CA's IT function pays close attention to how much of its time and effort is spent on ongoing operations, versus strategic projects, to the point of tracking this information in a time reporting application. "I would say as an organization, it is about a 70–30 split: 70 percent of the total time spent by the organization is on operational issues; 30 percent is more moving up from the tactical toward the strategic element," notes Phil. "If you looked at my boss or me and my direct peers, I would say the proportion is the other way round, which is just how it should be." Phil trusts his operational staff and seeks competent personnel to fill operational roles. Without this, he points out, "When you have got vice presidents and senior vice presidents spending a lot of their time on operational issues, that is an expensive way of running your operations."

Phil sees the process of determining which projects IT should implement as a joint effort between IT and business units. "Does the project have an ROI that is significant, or is it more around a compliance issue or something that we have to do?" is one of the first questions Phil asks. This is followed by assessing the risk of not taking action, and the readiness of the company to take the proposed action. If the company at large "isn't ready to take advantage of a particular technology or process, then you are wasting your time and effort on doing that." IT also must face a constantly full plate of projects. "There is a certain amount of advocacy and debate that goes on, because demand will always be greater than supply."

With projects vetted based on the previous criteria, Phil sees the decision-making process as critical to determining which projects to pursue. "Who the decision makers are needs to be specified very clearly up front. There are those who can have opinions, but there are only a few who can have a vote. And it needs to be very clear who the ones with a vote are, and what the rules of engagement are so that once the vote has been made, we act on it."

Phil devotes a large amount of his time to finding the right people for his organization, whether they are hired from the outside, or take a tour inside the IT organization as part of a program he is jointly developing with HR. While concrete skills may be required in specific cases, Phil initially looks at a more general set of criteria. "Potential employees don't necessarily have to have a proven track record in a particular discipline, but they have to have a proven track record of their ability to succeed, execute, and deliver. Execution is a critical factor. Combine execution with passion and I think everything else can be learned, frankly," said Phil.

Phil sees retention as a matter of giving people fulfilling work. "In my view, keeping good guys that you really want to keep long-term is generally about giving them really interesting stuff to do. I find the people who have the passion, and give them interesting, important things to do and give them accountability to do it, and more often than not they will stay." The market for competent employees is competitive, Phil comments, "You always have a discussion about salary and awards and recognition and so forth. Good workers generally know what they are worth better than you do. If you have got interesting stuff to give them to do, then they are going to hang around."

Phil sees a danger to performance management in IT, in the tendency to grade everyone in the middle. "I do advocate much more honesty in the way that we rank and evaluate people so that there is not this huge tendency to put everybody in the middle because that isn't true," said Phil. "There is only one person in the middle—everybody else is either above or below the middle—but the easy option is to group everybody in this lump of people who are doing okay. That is either not fair on the good people or fair on the people who are in the wrong position or doing the wrong role."

Phil notes that, "performance management is a culture," and that many organizations spend too much time looking at past performance rather than where a person wants to go in his or her career. "I think we do too much looking in the mirror, what have they done over the previous year, or years, and we need to do more around what is their potential in the future," said Phil. "It is a slightly different way of looking at it—looking forward rather than looking in the rear-view mirror."

Looking forward includes looking outside the confines of the IT organization for Phil. "That potential may well be outside the IT organization and that is okay. We are doing a lot of work with the HR department and ourselves about how we make it easier to be cross functional; have a part of your career in IT and maybe come back." While this may take a valuable resource away from IT in the short term, Phil sees this as creating better IT leaders in the long run. "Going back to what makes a successful leader in IT—a breadth of experience— maybe we should be able to provide that breadth of experience within the company. How cool would that be because you keep the skills— you keep the passion of the person. You don't necessarily lose them; you give them an interesting, varied, and broad career path and at the end of it you get potentially a very good business or IT leader." Phil envisions this process of working inside and outside the IT organization as occurring across business units and across geographies. "If you do that on a global basis; if you do that within the cultural restraints and the logistical restraints of a global company, then I think you have really cracked it."

Working for a global corporation can also have its drawbacks, especially when you are in one of the offices of a multinational outside its headquarters. "Like it or not, I work for an American company and it is driven out of the United States I think it is very easy to get into a 'them and us' situation, particularly if you are in the field," said Phil. "The challenge is to make sure that the needs and the requirements and the similarities and the exceptions that are within the global fields get back into the center; and ensure they are understood within the center; and the center is aware of and recognizes those changes."

The role does ensure Phil is well versed in business processes around the world, and can rapidly recognize similarities that can be leveraged across borders, and local differences that must be accommodated. "In many respects, being the international CIO is like being a conduit—you have to take the business requirements and the needs of the Asian, the European, the Latin American countries, and the markets that they operate in and their requirements; be they legal or statutory requirements; be they cultural requirements; be they market driven requirements—and make sure that those are heard, articulated, and presented in a fashion so that they are incorporated into whatever it is that we do." Often, Phil can discern differences that have no valid business purpose. "The example I always use is: 'Why do you need to do accounts payable differently in this country? That doesn't bring us any more sales of software; it just brings us additional complexity and costs.'" Phil sees this role of liaison between business units and geographies as a challenge, but an exciting one. "You could say it is being between a rock and a hard place, but I don't think that is the case. It is a really interesting position to be in, and an influential position to be in, in many respects."

Phil sees Breakthrough IT as being able to operate across multiple spheres, and taking into account the concerns of each member of the C-suite. "If you are trying to operate as a Breakthrough IT organization, you are addressing the controls; you are addressing governance; you are addressing costs; you are addressing efficiency and effectiveness; and you are addressing direction sensing and how technology can enable a business to go forward. So Breakthrough IT for me is being able to do all of it. If you don't get a buzz and excitement about this, then you are probably in the wrong job."

CHAPTER 10

Capitalizing on Success

Breakthrough IT is not an overnight success story. It is a long and complex process, and each step—from finding new sourcing options for continuing operations, to gradually refining the project portfolio—will be a test of a CEO's and CIO's ability, and of the capabilities of the organization as a whole. Like most worthwhile processes, Breakthrough IT becomes easier as momentum builds, and IT becomes an increasingly effective tool for value, growth, and competitive advantage. This will not happen overnight, of course, and applying Breakthrough IT to your company is expected to be an iterative process, continually refining the management of ongoing operations, gradually growing more competent at predicting the returns on a specific project, and using that information to refine the organization's selection of strategic projects.

The truly Breakthrough organization is not one that applies the methods in this book as a temporary mode of operating, but rather adopts these concepts and continually refines them, until they have the best IT shop in the business, perhaps one that is completely indistinguishable from the business units with which it collaborates. While this is a long and often difficult road, building a true Breakthrough IT organization is its own competitive weapon. Breakthrough IT is not something that can be bought from a vendor, discussed in a few training sessions, and forgotten; rather, it is like the preparation an elite athlete endures. For the athlete, like a company, there is no substitute for training and preparation, and when either enters the playing field, the one that has worked the hardest will prevail.

In the past several years, formerly mundane aspects of a business have become key strategic weapons. Operational areas as rudimentary as the supply chain have created retail giants, while manufacturing built around maximizing productivity is threatening stalwarts like the U.S. auto industry. While a well-managed IT organization built on the fundamentals of Breakthrough IT may not change the face of an entire industry, it does become one more weapon in the competitive arsenal, and one that is not easily duplicated, as it requires a cultural, personnel, and management shift.

Building Momentum

The area in which this cycle of continuous improvement will most dramatically be felt in the Breakthrough IT organization is in its ability to accurately predict returns on strategic projects. If IT can learn from every project, be it a total success or dramatic failure, it can build its knowledge in how to execute projects well, and more importantly how to determine the business benefit of each potential project, and choose the best projects to pursue. While competitors follow the latest technological or management fad, the Breakthrough IT shop can accurately predict the returns on a proposed project, ensure it dovetails with the company's strategy, and execute it within the estimated timeframe with the estimated cost. The individual competencies combine to create a massive competitive advantage, especially considering many of these projects can cost in the hundreds of millions of dollars and take years to implement. Even a small improvement in planning, execution, and recouping returns can translate into significant monetary value.

Critical to capturing this value is learning what goes right and wrong with every project. As mentioned in Chapter 1, human nature has us celebrate success and move on to capitalize on that success, and run from failure to avoid tarnishing our record. This will not do in the Breakthrough IT organization, and creating a culture in which success and failure are each analyzed and lessons learned are recorded and acted upon is a key to the process of continual learning.

These reviews should be conducted by IT, and in the C-suite and among business unit leaders as well. Strategic projects are a partnership between IT and a business unit, and if they are to deliver true value to the company, they should improve the processes behind a business unit rather than merely applying technology. Completed projects should be monitored for a defined period after they are implemented to ensure returns are being delivered, and see if change efforts were successful in migrating affected persons to the new way of doing business. In short, successfully implementing strategic projects does not end on go-live day.

Beyond Breakthrough IT

While true Breakthrough IT organizations are only beginning to appear, what is the next step in the evolution of IT that will affect them in the future? In general, IT will be the next supply chain, meaning that what started as a fairly mundane aspect of most businesses will become a source of competitive advantage, and a significant new market unto itself, creating specialized industries while changing the competitive landscape in one swoop. IT is poised for a similar renaissance, and Breakthrough IT will lay the foundation for further change in this area. IT at most corporations is a mundane aspect of the business, and the first company that truly gets it right is in a position to leverage its IT shop much as some of the retail giants have leveraged their supply chain to their advantage.

Several significant trends will shape the future of the Breakthrough IT organization:

- The continued commoditization of business applications
- The shift toward decentralized IT
- IT in product design, and as a freestanding product
- The mastery of business data

Continued Commoditization

Commoditized business applications have already changed the IT landscape. No longer is the company with the most skilled engineers and best programmers able to produce a unique application that serves as a tool for competitive advantage. Even the most complex business applications—from integrated logistics or accounting, to customer relationship management—can be purchased off the shelf.

This trend is moving in an even more granular direction, with software companies producing small applications targeted at a very specific purpose—producing invoices, for example. Rather than turning to an application vendor for a monolithic package covering an entire business, companies can buy tiny components and connect each to form customized business systems built from commodity building blocks. This will dramatically change the IT landscape, as it is no longer a question of how well you can implement a large software package, but how well you can connect the various commodity building blocks and arrange them for maximum business value.

This change should further speed the deployment of enterprise applications, since blocks of functionality can be implemented independently of other blocks, at the same time allowing for very interesting sourcing options. If your business applications are composed of these interconnected blocks of functionality, it suddenly becomes very easy to replace one block with a hosted application, or "drop in" a vendor's logistics application that completely changes your physical supply chain without affecting the systems or processes that support it. Assuming some level of standardization between each of these building blocks, once-complex tasks such as integrating another company's systems with a new parent company or spinning off a business unit will become vastly easier.

This modularized IT world will increase the number of vendors already offering hosted applications, and perhaps the most interesting change is that virtual companies can be formed overnight by purchasing commodity building blocks and integrating them in a new and interesting manner. A small business will be able to connect to a world-class fulfillment center, while a massive corporation can quickly integrate a mom-and-pop store into its distribution chain to get more information about the sales of its products. The IT staffer will increasingly become an architect, rather than a specialized engineer, and business leaders will no longer need to know the nuances behind business systems, as they can instead focus on assembling blocks of functionality to meet their business needs.

To Centralize or Not to Centralize?

Another issue the Breakthrough IT organization will encounter is the continuing debate between centralizing IT and decentralizing, perhaps even to the point of disbanding the traditional "freestanding" IT entity altogether. When the PC first hit the corporation, its introduction was often spearheaded by individual business units that would install one or two machines, and use them for very specific applications relevant to that department. As the PC became more commonplace, sheer numbers made a compelling case for centralized management, and with the desire to consolidate business data and applications, one centralized IT organization made sense. However, as business software continues to become a series of connected components rather than monolithic applications, individual business units may be in the best position to determine and manage the components that are appropriate to them. IT will shift toward a process and architect role, designing the overall system and determining the inputs and outputs of each component, while individual business units with the most detailed understanding of their particular function will choose and implement the components that are most appropriate to their specific process. No longer will changes in one area of the business dramatically affect other areas, assuming a central body can ensure inputs and outputs remain consistent.

While IT will likely lose its total control over corporate technology and no longer play a role in managing each and every application that exists within the corporation, it will become increasingly involved in gaining a holistic understanding of the processes that keep the business running. Pushing detailed technical knowledge down to the line level in the corporation can also create cost savings, as those closest to a process also have the ability to identify areas for improvement that might otherwise be overlooked.

Key to decentralization is clear lines of communication between each business unit and the CIO. Decentralized models that have failed are often characterized by many distinct fiefdoms, independent groups with their own technology, strategy, and vision without regard for any standards or integration with the rest of the company. A successful decentralized IT organization should be one in which common tools and empowerments are spread throughout the organization to implement a shared and coordinated vision.

IT will determine how to connect and leverage each process at a macro level to achieve the corporation's objectives. While the CIO will lose some element of the control he or she enjoys today, that person will also become more of a relationship builder, and become more valuable in guiding the business and executing on the company's strategy.

IT Inside—IT as a Product

The idea that different business units can act as a component of nearly every business process has been gaining ground—from the embedding of financial and accounting rigor into all aspects of a business during the manufacturing revolution, to more modern concepts like design for manufacturability and embedding marketing in product design. It is increasingly clear that embedding multiple perspectives into product design vastly improves the quality of the end product. IT has largely stayed outside of the traditional product design process, in the worst case hearing about a new product only when some unique aspect of that product broke a current system or process and IT was summoned to fix it only as an afterthought. In the future, IT will be involved in product design, and perhaps even be sold as a standalone product to external customers.

Involving IT in product design is both highly beneficial and risky. Internal users of IT are generally a captive audience. No one is going to buy his or her own computer for use at work, or build his or her own internal e-mail system. Internal users also are far more forgiving of any problems or deficiencies of internal systems, since they essentially get access to these systems for free as part of their employment. IT is a monopoly to internal users, with all the good and bad traits associated with monopolies.

External customers, on the other hand, have invested both time and money in purchasing a product or service, and generally have an array of options when choosing a new product or service. These users expect and demand a high level of service from the technology components of a product or service, in terms of both reliability and availability, and often demand a standard most internal IT organizations are not accustomed to meeting.

On the positive side, this high level of service can bring a new standard of excellence to an IT organization that benefits its external and internal customers. Customer applications also benefit from the rapid feedback of a group that has a choice in which products and services it uses, and can vote with its money. Whereas a new ERP system may be met with lukewarm acceptance by internal users since it is the only game in town, a high-quality feature on a product will be rapidly recognized by external customers. This rapid feedback can improve both the product and any internal systems, and an increasingly open dialogue with end customers and the company can lead to increased sales and better relationships if properly managed.

An obvious area for IT involvement in product design is the increasing number of products that directly use technology as one of their components. From consumer products that "phone home" for software and feature updates, to business-to-business communications that facilitate the use and maintenance of a physical product, or provide an ancillary service, IT is a key feature and design component of these products. Unfortunately, these IT features are often designed without consideration of a company's IT environment as a whole, either by a subsection of a product design team or by a few dedicated IT staffers who focus solely on designing products and are not involved with IT's other activities. This results in product-specific systems and processes that do not leverage internal systems or data that might already be available. The systems that cater to external customers may not exchange data with internal systems, missing the potential to gather detailed information about the customers and their interaction with the organization's products, which can be repackaged and used by every business unit from marketing to accounts receivable.

Perhaps even more interesting to the Breakthrough IT organization is offering IT services as a standalone product. Supply chain leaders like Wal-Mart have been doing this for years, offering suppliers visibility into Wal-Mart's internal systems to gather data from the point of sale, allowing suppliers to plan their production around what Wal-Mart's customers are buying. Other companies have packaged an internal process or system into a product that can then be placed on the market, from Six Sigma and other process improvement methodologies to consulting organizations that grew from a high-quality internal IT department.

IT-based products need not be as dramatic as a new methodology and cadre of experts to support it. Rather, simple visibility into your organization's systems similar to Wal-Mart's practice can create a more efficient process for you and a valuable product for an external customer. The easiest place to start is looking at current systems and processes, and searching for those that might be valuable to an external customer. Many manufacturing organizations have detailed production planning and tracking systems as a matter of course. Offering visibility to your manufacturing process could prove highly valuable to your end customers, and can be presented with few changes to internal systems. You must remain cognizant of the fact that external customers will have vastly higher support demands and standards than internal users, even if the systems are identical. A recorded message from support at 5:10 P.M. may satisfy an employee while destroying a valuable customer relationship.

A Breakthrough IT organization is poised to contribute to product design, and look for ways its own systems and processes can be packaged as a product. With ongoing operational processes properly sourced, and solid relationships in the C-suite, the Breakthrough CIO has the focus and insight into organizational strategy to determine where IT can truly transition from an ongoing cost to a profit center.

Who Has the Data?

The other sweeping trend in corporate IT will be a better ability to generate knowledge and understanding from business data. With the ready availability of data warehousing applications, and their adoption by many businesses, there are reams of data in most corporations—from transactional data spanning multiple years, to competitive and marketing information culled from other organizations or internal research. While many companies are quite good at gathering this data and performing rudimentary analyses, few can translate this into true business knowledge that generates competitive advantage.

Companies have been looking at data acquisition as a technical problem for too long, seeing an ability to acquire all kinds of data and produce stacks of reports as the ultimate goal, rather than being able to analyze data to make more effective business decisions. The modern corporation has perfected the art of capturing snapshots of various business functions, and providing detailed trend analysis, but for all this data to be truly valuable it must provide diagnostic and proactive reporting. For example, most businesses are able to monitor their logistics operations, and provide detailed reporting on fulfillment rates, shipments, and delays. While this reporting is helpful, it does not provide true intelligence—in this case, looking at the entire supply chain and predicting shipment delays due to manufacturing or supplier shortages while there is still time to react to avoid the delay.

The next phase of business reporting will provide a view of an entire business process, across traditional departments or business units. While some of this cross-functional reporting has come into common use at the executive level, providing dashboards or "snapshot" reports that deliver an overview of the entire company, it has rarely made its way down to the line level. If finance or production had true visibility into sales, for example, functions that occur at the end of a business transaction can actively plan and schedule their resources, based on what is happening at the beginning of the business transaction, rather than constantly acting in a reactive mode.

Companies that can consolidate multiple reports, ad-hoc spreadsheets, and other consolidation tools, and transition specialized interpretive ability into single dashboard or "active" reports will be able to make better business decisions. Reporting that feeds into planning and decision making will slowly replace reporting that is used to diagnose current problems, or look at historical data that is fed into a complex, manual analysis process to feed a decision about the future.

The Future of the CIO Role

The CIO role has reached a crossroads. Initially defined as a "keeper of the technology" and little else, the CIO of a Breakthrough IT organization clearly departs from that role. The C-suite in general is in the midst of a transition, as world events and changing views on the nature of the corporation have engendered a slew of new C-level titles. Some of these new positions are little more than glorified managerial roles, and as time progresses, the people who fill these roles must be able to make the case that they can work with the traditional business leaders like the CEO and CFO to understand, contribute to, and execute the corporation's strategy. This will be the litmus test for C-level roles, and a shakedown in the proliferation of C titles will likely happen in the next decade. While the CIO has the benefit of a longer historical presence, he or she will be subject to the same scrutiny as other, newer roles.

The CIO of a Breakthrough IT organization has effectively moved beyond a technology-focused role, and assumed more of a process-driven role. Rather than maintaining infrastructure, the Breakthrough CIO maintains and improves processes. Some organizations have already felt the need for such a role and have created *chief process officers* or the like. While the need is acute, the CIO is in a better position to assume a process-focused role rather than attempting to create an entirely new position and support organization.

However, this new sensitivity to business process does represent a threat to the old-style CIO. The technical CIO position in its traditional guise will lose importance as organizations become process-oriented and technology becomes more of a commodity, where a process expert can connect freestanding pieces of business functionality with minimal concern for the underlying technology. The CIO who does not assume this process role will likely be amalgamated under a CPO-type role, or continue to be a subordinate of an operating or financial officer. The traditional role of the CIO as a pure technologist will disappear, and those CIOs who do not evolve with the times will disappear with it.

This changing business environment does present some risk to the CIO, and a corresponding opportunity. Several years ago, the CIO position was the end of the line for a technology manager, who was rarely considered for any other C-level position. As CIOs assume more responsibility for translating business strategy into process changes and optimizations, the role is becoming a proving ground for future C-level roles. As the CIO position loses its technology stigma, it is also becoming a respected position that attracts nontechnical business-people, increasing the competitiveness of the role and the advancement potential of the position. The CIO is on the forefront of this C-suite shakeup, and one who has built his or her organization and career around the principles of Breakthrough IT is poised to become a more valuable business leader as the top positions in the company become increasingly open to him or her.

In Closing

Breakthrough IT may be one of the most difficult transitions a company's IT function ever undertakes, but it will also likely be one of the most rewarding. For the CEO and board of directors, Breakthrough IT is a source of competitive advantage that is both difficult to duplicate and extremely powerful in that the Breakthrough IT organization is directly involved with the determination and execution of the business's strategy. For the CIO, he or she is no longer a technologist relegated to a purely operational role and under constant pressure to deliver commodity services at ever-lower prices.

The CIO position in the Breakthrough IT shop is that of a true business leader, attractive to businesspeople without a pure technology background and a possible proving ground for future CEOs, CFOs, and COOs.

Employees of the Breakthrough IT organization also benefit from its transition. Technical competence is rapidly becoming a commodity, and today's hot new application or technology is tomorrow's commodity. An employee of a Breakthrough IT organization is no longer forced into chasing after "the next big thing," and is expected to develop business process expertise, a skill relevant both inside and outside an IT organization. IT employees and business unit employees speak the same language in the Breakthrough IT organization, and rather than a subservient customer service model, the Breakthrough IT employee and business unit employee partner to produce excellent business processes that serve to increase the capabilities of the corporation at large.

After laying the foundation of Breakthrough IT at a company, IT can move far beyond its traditional role. The Breakthrough IT shop can contribute to product design, or perhaps sell access to internal systems or expertise as a standalone product. Transparent and flexible business processes, combined with commodity business software "building blocks," will allow companies to rapidly integrate acquisitions or create virtual companies nearly instantaneously to accommodate market or strategy changes.

As the competitive landscape shifts, Breakthrough IT provides a solid organizational platform on which to shape your company to react to these changes. It may not be a magic bullet, or a change that can be implemented with a few meetings and slideshows, but Breakthrough IT will truly allow the IT function to deliver unprecedented organizational value. I wish you the best of success with your journey toward Breakthrough IT.

ACTION POINTS

Action points provide concrete steps you can use to begin implementing ideas from this chapter. For this chapter, the action points are:

- Check the success of Breakthrough IT in your organization. Where does your IT shop stand on the evolution from an engineering function, to a utility, to a true Breakthrough IT shop?

- Develop a set of performance metrics and review with C-suite colleagues to evaluate your IT organization in the context of Breakthrough IT. Look for ways to continually improve IT and further the transition to Breakthrough status.

- Look for opportunities for IT to participate in product development, either providing input into products that include technology-centric features or selling your internal IT services as a standalone product. Investigate the profit potential and required sales and support structures for selling IT as a product.

- Investigate your current data-gathering capabilities, and look for ways to leverage the large amounts of data most organizations capture into analytical tools that go beyond mere reporting. Rather than detailing the past, leverage your data to predict the future and provide early warnings and indicators of market conditions and how they affect your company.

- Make your IT and business processes more portable and transparent, so they are best able to take advantage of future technologies that may allow for off-the-shelf "component" applications. This portability also allows for rapid sourcing changes, adaptation to new technologies, and flexibility in the case of mergers and acquisitions.

- Consider using the CIO role as a leadership development position, for those both inside and outside IT. The CIO role in a Breakthrough IT organization has a strong focus on operational, financial, and strategy execution disciplines, and is often overlooked as a potential CEO-development role.

 EXECUTIVE SUMMARY

Breakthrough IT is not a simple activity that can be "done" to an organization; rather, it is a continual process of transition, improvement, and refinement, with the ultimate goal of IT providing accurate, predictable returns on IT investment. This process is gradually refined and improved as the IT organization transitions its focus from ongoing operations, and learns from the success and failure of strategic projects. Perhaps the ultimate testament to the success of Breakthrough IT is when the CIO position is respected by fellow C-suite colleagues and considered a proving ground for potential CFO, COO, and even CEO candidates, rather than the end to a long technical career.

As an organization perfects its ability to execute on projects and deliver the expected business benefit, several future opportunities exist as the Breakthrough IT organization looks for new ways to produce business value. Moving toward well-understood and "portable" business processes allows the IT organization to take advantage of new technologies that promise off-the-shelf business applications, packaged into individual components. This allows the

EXECUTIVE SUMMARY (CONTINUED)

organization to rapidly shift its processes to different software, providers, and geographic locations to take advantage of market conditions, and rapidly integrate acquired companies or quickly create new business entities.

Increased data analysis capabilities are another trend Breakthrough IT organizations will take advantage of. IT has long been capable of gathering and reporting on the massive amounts of transactional and customer data that passes through its systems, but most of these reports are focused on the past, effectively keeping score. Businesses that are able to use past data to predict the future will have an undeniable source of competitive advantage versus those businesses that use their data solely to report the past.

Perhaps the most interesting trend in the future of IT is the use of IT in product development. Most products and services have an increasing amount of technology integrated into them, either as a feature or core component of the product. Internal IT organizations that have excellent processes and data may also be the source of standalone products, turning IT into a true profit center.

Index

217